D1453832

Like Beads
on a String

Like Beads on a String

A Culture History of the Seminole Indians in Northern Peninsular Florida

Brent Richards Weisman

The University of Alabama Press
Tuscaloosa and London

Library of Congress Cataloging-in-Publication Data

Weisman, Brent Richards, 1952–
  Like beads on a string.

  Bibliography: p.
  Includes index.
  1. Seminole Indians—History.   2. Seminole Indians—Social life and
customs.   3. Indians of North America—Florida—History.   4. Indians
of North America—Florida—Social life and customs.   I. Title.
E99.S28W43   1989   975.9′00497   88-5765
ISBN 0-8173-0411-8 (alk. paper)

British Library Cataloguing-in-Publication Data available

To my grandfather

Contents

Preface

Florida's Seminole Indians are an increasingly visible minority of the state's population. The issues that continue to place them in the public eye include high-stakes bingo, state and federal litigation concerning native land and water rights, and land claims suits brought by the Indians against both the state and the federal governments. Anthropologists have been and continue to be intrigued by the apparent survival in contemporary Seminole culture of traditional southeastern aboriginal religious customs (Capron 1953; Sturtevant 1954; Buswell 1972), social practices (Stirling 1935; Spoehr 1941, 1944; Garbarino 1972), and political patterns (King 1978), while popular treatments of the last of Florida's native Americans (Mathiessen 1984) deftly portray their struggles in a world not entirely of their making.

Two themes recur in the ethnographic literature on the Seminoles. First, there is the observation that, while the core of Seminole culture has remained conservative, Seminole Indians exhibit a remarkable ability to change and innovate. Thus the old is balanced with the new. The second observation pertains to the high respect for individual rights granted in Seminole society. This respect is illustrated in the following story, collected from a reservation Seminole in recent years: "One man of the Bear Clan and the other man of the Snake Clan were the first men to get interested in the white man's ways. They joined the soldiers and they were learning how to speak English, but the Indians didn't mind. Everybody had a right to do what they pleased to do, so they didn't care. They were just doing what they wanted to do" (King 1978:18).

In the words of another resident of the Big Cypress reservation, "everyone should be left alone to do what he wants. Neighbor should not interfere with neighbor, and no one should tell anyone else what to do" (Garbarino 1972:99). These qualities have clearly combined to spell success for the Seminoles of today. Yet the lasting impression of Seminole culture is one of enigma and mystery. The following report of the induction of the new Miccosukee tribal chairman in 1985 demonstrates that the Indians themselves are partly responsible for this mystique:

To honor Mr. Billie [the inductee] in a traditional ceremony of gift presentation and wishing, Seminole chief, James E. Billie, dressed in traditional dress of the long shirt, leggings and turban, poled his dugout from deep in the Everglades to the Miccosukee Reservation where [he arrived] before hundreds of tribal members, employees, dignitaries and honored guests. Media from all over the state were on hand to record the historical event. Chairman Jim Billie presented the newly elected Chief with three gifts to demonstrate "power." The first of the three gifts represents "power" as used in the "power of the pen." With that, he presented Chief Billie with a pen. The second gift was presented in the Miccosukee language. Chairman Billie chose not to translate to the public, but reported to the *Seminole Tribune* that it is the "green power that makes the world go 'round."

The third and most powerful in the eyes of the head medicine-man, Sonny Billie [the inductee], was a panther hide. Chief [James] Billie explained that the panther has a powerful medicine in the claws and tail, and is used for medicine at the Miccosukee-

> Seminole Green Corn Dance—the two yearly week-long tribal re-
> ligious ceremonies held in Miccosukee. The two chiefs pledged
> friendship and unity between the two tribes. [Billie 1985]

The drama of the scene was no doubt heightened by James Billie's immediate flight back to the Everglades aboard a helicopter.

Does history have a role to play in helping us understand contemporary Seminole culture? If so, do the Seminoles have a history independent of Euro-American documentation? If in fact a
Seminole culture history can be produced, what major themes
will it exhibit? What have the Seminoles themselves imparted to
these themes, and what antecedent processes have influenced
their development? The present study will address these and
other questions.

The foundations of Seminole culture rest in the institutions of
late prehistoric Mississippian societies of the lower Southeast.
Mississippian societies were organized into chiefdoms, in which
a triad of distinct but integrated religious cults provided social
cohesion (Knight 1986). Economies were diverse, but in the interior riverine floodplains, emphasis was on maize agriculture
(Muller 1987:13). The settlement pattern was organized in a
nested hierarchy of political and economic affiliation through
which redistribution and forms of exchange linked single-family
homesteads (Brose 1980), hamlets, local centers, and primary
mound centers, or "capitals." The primary seat of economic production was the family or lineage (Muller 1987:20).

The Creek Indians and other Muskogean-speaking groups of
the historic period were the immediate heirs of the institutions
of Mississippian culture. While the historical circumstances of
European contact in the sixteenth century did much to transform aboriginal society, religious practices (Knight 1986:683),
settlement patterns (Swanton 1928b), and economic systems
(Muller 1987:14) clearly link the historic Muskogeans with the
Mississippian cultures known through archaeology.

Although the eighteenth century Seminoles in Florida were
undeniably Creek in origin (Sturtevant 1971) and political affiliation (Doster 1974, Wright 1986), there are also signs of an emer-
gent ethnicity through which the Seminoles freed themselves of

their allegiance to their homeland. The development of this ethnicity greatly complicated colonial relations on the southern frontier and eventually became a decisive factor in the U.S. government's creation of an Indian policy. To show how this Seminole ethnogenesis came about, the present culture history will evaluate the complementary roles of culture, history, and the individual in effecting Seminole ethnicity.

Acknowledgments

This book had its beginnings early in 1983, when I had a brief conversation with Jerald T. Milanich, curator in archaeology at the Florida State Museum, Gainesville. Milanich had just met with Donald Sheppard and William Goza, who carried with them a 147-year-old diary describing and depicting the Second Seminole War camp of the famed Seminole warrior Osceola, also known as Powell. Sheppard and Goza were certain that diary clues would permit the archaeologists to find the Powell's Town site, and in fact they had already obtained permission from the Edwards family, owners of the Flying Eagle Ranch near Inverness, Florida, to search the alleged area of the site. Goza, president of the philanthropic Wentworth Foundation, was eager to provide Milanich with the initial funding necessary to carry out the archaeological survey. Milanich proceeded to look for a graduate student to serve as his assistant on the project. Would I be willing to tackle the Osceola site and possibly parlay it into a dissertation? With little hesitation I accepted the offer and soon found myself on the course that was to lead to the completion of my dissertation under Milanich's direction some four years later.

Many individuals and institutions deserve mention for their roles in the development of the field project, and I thank many others for their guidance in the revision of the dissertation and in the subsequent preparation of this book. Jerald Milanich contributed significantly to both endeavors and deserves special recognition for his wisdom, savvy, and support.

I thank Lucille and Frank Coggeshall for sharing with me their knowledge regarding the history of the Prince diary. Other individuals who have made unique contributions to the project include Donald Sheppard, Paul Anderson, and Lynn DeLong, all of Inverness, Florida, William Dayton of Dade City, and Al and Bev Hansen of Spring Hill. Landowners who graciously allowed us to carry out our fieldwork include Phil Zellner, Lloyd and Shirley Newman, Dan Edwards and the Edwards family, and the South Florida Council of the Boy Scouts of America. The able volunteers of the Withlacoochee River Archaeology Council helped immeasurably in the archaeological survey and excavations in the Citrus County area.

Funding for the project came from the following sources, listed here in roughly chronological order: the Florida State Museum, the Wentworth Foundation, the Inverness Rotary Club, the Florida State Museum Associates, the Florida Department of State, Division of Historical Resources, a benefactor of Citrus County archaeology, and the Department of Anthropology of the University of Florida, whose award of the 1986 John M. Goggin Memorial Fellowship allowed me to complete my dissertation.

My doctoral committee—which included Milanich as chair, anthropologists Barbara Purdy, Michael Moseley, and Allan Burns, and historian John Mahon—all made important suggestions for improvement of the manuscript before its final submission in January 1987. Guy Prentice drafted a number of the figures and provided other technical suggestions. The transition from dissertation to book was greatly eased by Judith Knight, chief editor for The University of Alabama Press. Two anonymous reviewers provided thoughtful criticisms of the original manuscript, which was revised and much improved in line with their suggestions.

Finally, I thank my family and dear friends, who tolerated what must have appeared at times to be sheer nonsense and who trusted that eventually sense would come.

Like Beads
on a String

Introduction

North Peninsular Florida

This book primarily considers the historical archaeology of the Seminole Indians in north peninsular Florida. The north peninsula and the region of the Florida panhandle in the vicinity of Tallahassee were the two major centers of early Seminole settlement. There are indications that the Europeans of the time were more familiar with the Seminoles of the Tallahassee Red Hills than with the bands inhabiting the more remote regions of the Suwannee River drainage and the Alachua savanna, yet the archaeological picture of the panhandle bands is vastly incomplete. The north peninsula Seminoles did not entirely escape documentary notice, nor is their archaeology entirely unknown. The reason is in part the site survey and reconnaissance sponsored by the University of Florida in the vicinity of the Gainesville campus, near the former heartland of the peninsular Seminoles. The north peninsula is also a favorable area for study because Seminole occupation there was continuous for almost a century, whereas the panhandle groups were effectively removed from the area through combined American and Creek hostilities in the early decades of the nineteenth century. Thus Seminole archaeological sites found in the north peninsula usefully illustrate several significant trends in the development of Seminole culture history.

The study area is bounded on the west by the drainage of the Suwannee River, on the east by the St. Johns River, on the south

1

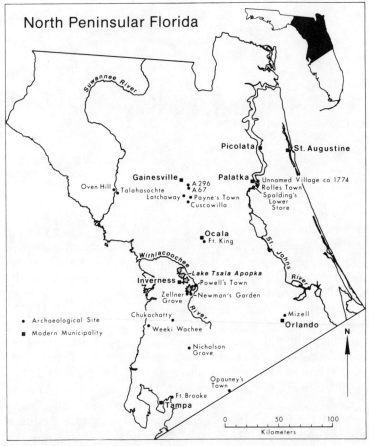

Figure 1. Location of the study area

by a line extending from Tampa Bay northeastward to the head-waters of the St. Johns River (approximately 28 degrees north latitude), and on the north by a line east-west across the peninsula at approximately 30 degrees north latitude. The study area and the major archaeological sites discussed in the text are illustrated in figure 1.

Previous prehistoric archaeology in the north peninsula has

Table 1. Important historical events in north peninsular Florida through 1765

1765	Treaty of Picolata. Indians cede territory east of the St. Johns River to the British.
1740	Cowkeeper assists Ogelthorpe in attack on Spanish St. Augustine. Beginnings of Alachua Seminole.
1710	Creeks use peninsula for slave raiding and as hunting ground.
1702	English and Creek raids destroy Florida missions.
1690	Florida missions in decline.
1656	Timucuan rebellion against Spanish missions.
1607–1655	Proliferation of Spanish (Franciscan) missions; dramatic change in aboriginal lifeways.
1565	Pedro Menedez de Aviles explores the St. Johns River south to Lake George.
1564	Intertribal warfare among Timucua aided by Frenchman Laudonnière.
1539	Soto entrada travels overland through heart of peninsula. Decline of aboriginal populations.
1528	Landing of Pánfilo de Narváez, Tampa Bay.
1000–1528	The development of aboriginal Timucuan chiefdoms. Alachua Tradition and Safety Harbor archaeological cultures.

been neatly summarized by Milanich and Fairbanks (1980:24–26,28–33), who divided the region into four archaeological culture areas. According to the authors, the last aboriginal occupation in three of the areas (the fourth is the central Gulf coast, in the vicinity of Tampa Bay) was by bands of Seminole Indians, whose migrations into the region can be traced in the archaeological record. Table 1 presents important culture-historical events in the north peninsula through 1765.

Geography is of some importance in any consideration of the cultural adaptation of the Seminoles to north peninsular Florida. Two of the three major rivers in the province—the Suwannee and the Withlacoochee—empty into the Gulf of Mexico and thus provided important river routes for Seminole commerce with

Spanish Cuba. River travel by the Seminoles was of particular concern when Florida was under British and American control, for both of these powers wanted to prevent the Indians from engaging in uncontrolled trade with foreign sources. The Americans in particular took precautions against waterborne Indian trade by establishing in 1823 an Indian reservation with boundaries well inland from the Gulf. The British, however, used the St. Johns River to their advantage and established several major Indian trading houses on its banks deep within the Seminole domain.

Site survey information suggests that the first Seminole settlements in the north peninsula were located in the scattered oak-hickory uplands, especially in regions bordering the Alachua savanna. South of the Alachua area, the first settlements were located on the Brooksville Ridge, a narrow spine of highland tending north-northwest from present-day Brooksville (Hernando County) to the Withlacoochee gap at Dunellon (Marion County).

Sites are shallow, usually with a single component, and are often found near late prehistoric sites of the Alachua tradition (in the Alachua area) or, south of the Withlacoochee, near sites of the Safety Harbor archaeological culture. It is rare for Seminole sites to occur as upper components in prehistoric shell middens because the lifeways of the Seminoles did not at first emphasize the collecting of riverine and aquatic food resources. However, the Seminoles did not abandon the use of native-made pottery until their ultimate move into the southern Florida glades, and so their distinctive "brushed" ceramics are diagnostic of their presence on northern Florida sites.[1]

The number of known Seminole archaeological sites is small, especially compared with the numbers of sites upon which archaeologists customarily define cultures or phases. Because the sites are frequently of low artifact density, they often go undiscovered and are inadvertently destroyed through various human activities. Seminole sites rarely have above-ground manifestations and must be discovered through a detailed direct-historic approach. Thus their identification is both costly and labor intensive. These factors have tended to discourage systematic, problem-oriented research. Also, the relative wealth of documentary information pertaining to the political history of the Seminoles has eclipsed the importance of a social history derived from archaeology. The Seminoles themselves have not as yet placed a high priority on the archaeological investigation of their past, for understandable reasons. It is hoped, however, that this circumstance will change, with Seminole archaeology playing a major role in the development of a Seminole-derived culture history. It is also hoped that scholars of southeastern archaeology and ethnohistory will bring Seminole studies into the mainstream of their concerns.

Previous Views of the Seminole Past

Most previous interpretations of Seminole culture history have favored one of three approaches: a political model, an adaptational model, or an anthropological model. Political models emphasize the importance of the Euro-American presence in the colonial Southeast and its influence on the direction of Seminole culture history. Treaties, land cessions, and trading policies between colonists and Indians are featured as catalysts for change in aboriginal society. The primary proponent of this view was Charles H. Fairbanks (1974, 1978) of the University of Florida. Adaptational approaches hold that environmental and ecological conditions exerted selection pressure on the culture pattern of the Seminoles, a pressure that favored the development of new adaptive strategies and the abandonment of some older ones. Thus as the Seminoles moved into different environmental niches in the Florida peninsula, different responses were called for. The combination of these responses into a new cultural pattern essentially signaled the ethnic transformation from Creek to Seminole. This view appears in the work of Craig and Peebles (1974) and also characterized some of Fairbanks's publications. Anthropological perspectives emphasize the continuity between Creek and Seminole cultures through time (Sturtevant 1971) and illuminate the development of new cultural institutions with reference to preceding cultural forms. Ta-

Table 2. A comparison of Seminole culture histories.

Year	Fairbanks	Craig/Peebles	Sturtevant	BRW
1880	modern crystalization		new ethnogenesis	
1870				
1860			isolation	
1850		subtropical adaptation		
1840	withdrawal			
1830		foraging		revitalization
1820			warfare, separation	
1810		hamlet farming		
1800				
1790	resistance, removal			
1780				
1770	separation			enterprise
1760				
1750				
1740		pastoralism		
1730				
1720	colonization		proto-Seminole	colonization
1710				

Sources: Fairbanks (1978); Craig and Peebles (1974); Sturtevant (1971).

ble 2 summarizes these interpretations of Seminole culture history, including the approach outlined in the present volume.

The major ethnohistorical study of the Florida Seminoles was done by Charles Fairbanks in 1957 at the request of the Indian Claims Section of the U.S. Department of Justice in response to a petition filed in 1950 by certain southern Florida Seminoles against the United States, under terms provided in the Indian Claims Commission Act of 1946. These individuals sought financial compensation for the loss of approximately 32 million acres of Florida lands to the United States between 1823 and 1835.[2] Based on the principle of aboriginal possession, the Seminole claim asserted that the Indians' ancestors had resided in Florida "from time immemorial" and had relinquished their lands only under duress.

The claims of the suit suggested three avenues of ethnohistorical research available to the Indian Claims Commission. First, the Indian claim that their tribal rights to property had been recognized by the Spaniards at the time of their cession of Florida to the United States could be confirmed or denied by referring to articles of Spanish colonial law. Second, the antiquity of Florida's Seminoles had to be established on the basis of available documentation. Finally, because the suit contended that the Seminole Tribe had been deprived of its lands without compensation, the existence of a Seminole polity at the time of American possession of Florida needed verification.

The report addressed the last two concerns.[3] Fairbanks's conclusions indicated that the earliest Seminoles to reside in Florida permanently were the Oconee Creeks, who had migrated to the Alachua savanna by 1738, and, at the same time, lower Creek Mikasukis, who settled in the vicinity of Tallahassee. These conclusions did not differ significantly from knowledge gathered in the previous century (Swan in Schoolcraft 1851–1857: vol. 5:260; Gatschet 1884:68). Fairbanks adopted the following scenario for the settlement of Florida by the Seminoles. British-assisted Lower Creek raids in 1702–1704 against the Spanish-Indian mission chain in north Florida effectively exterminated the last of the Florida aborigines and left the Spaniards on the Atlantic coast of Florida with an unprotected rear. Into this void came bands of Lower Creeks, whose homes had been along the streams of central Georgia and in the Chattahoochee River basin to the west. Those that settled in the Tallahassee Red Hills and on the Apalachicola apparently did so at the request of the Spaniards, while others, including the Alachua band of Oconees who settled closest to Spanish St. Augustine, were decidedly pro-British in sympathy. Thus the stage was set for the development of factionalism among the new Indians of Florida.

A more controversial conclusion of the Fairbanks report indicated that the Seminoles had in fact established an independent polity that was in place by the year 1800. The formation of the polity had been influenced by favorable trade relations between the Seminoles and the British overlords of Florida (between the years 1763 and 1783), which promoted a schism between the Florida Seminoles and the Creek Nation to the north. The implication of this finding for the Indian Claims case was clear. By the time of formal American rule of the peninsula in 1821, the Seminole Nation was well established as a political entity. Furthermore, the oral testimony provided by John M. Goggin on behalf of the Seminoles indicated that Spanish colonial law had in fact recognized limited Indian rights to Florida lands.[4] According to the Spanish view, individual Indians and their families held claim to their farms and villages, while hunting territories were in the public domain.

The Indian Claims Commission found for the Seminoles, and on April 27, 1976, entered a final award of $16 million to the Nation.[5] The award was meant to be distributed among the descendants of all those Indians living in Florida on September 18, 1823, the date of the Treaty of Moultrie Creek. This meant division of the sum four ways: to the Seminole Nation of Oklahoma, whose ancestors were Seminoles deported from Florida; to the Seminole Tribe of Florida and the Miccosukee Tribe of Florida, both federally recognized tribes descended from the original Florida Seminoles; and to the remaining Seminoles in Florida of no tribal affiliation.[6] However, no equitable means of distributing the funds has been devised, and the monies remain undelivered.[7]

The Fairbanks report and the Indian Claims testimony together worked to emphasize the complexity of Seminole ethnohistory while embedding it inextricably in the politics of tribalism. Earlier works had ably summarized the diverse tribal origins of the Seminoles, their linguistic division into Muskogee and Mikasuki-speaking bands, and the chronology of their arrivals in Florida (Swanton 1922, 1946). But now for the first time Indians and whites alike were evaluating this history to determine its utility in practical affairs. However, definitive histories of the Seminole, Mikasuki, and Oklahoma nations remain to be written.

With the Indian Claims research as a foundation, Fairbanks (1978) later proposed a formal outline of Seminole culture history. Unlike the previous study, this work incorporated the limited data then available from archaeology. Five periods or phases were described through the course of which Seminole ethnicity progressively developed in response to changing political, ecological, and social conditions.[8] In Fairbanks's view, the evolution from Creek to Seminole was a case study in culture change.

The Seminoles of the colonization phase (1716–1763; Fairbanks 1978:169) were removed from their former contacts in the Creek Nation and remote from the mercantilism of the British-inspired deerskin trade. There was accordingly a reduced need for political centralization. Seminole towns, such as they were, were constructed without a central squareground, were not permanent in nature, and did not serve as a unifying element for outlying populations. The Seminole settlement pattern thus clearly diverged from the Creek. In addition, the Seminoles of the Alachua savanna began herding the free-ranging cattle descended from the Spanish stock of the La Chua ranch. This pastoralism further reinforced changes away from settled, permanent village life.

In Fairbanks's estimation, women's roles remained relatively unaffected by the processes of social and economic change, and so their continued manufacture of Chattahoochee Brushed pottery (Bullen 1950; Goggin 1958) linked the Seminole and Creek ceramic traditions. Like their Seminole counterparts, Creek women were also responsible for conservative elements in colonial-era aboriginal society (Fairbanks 1962:51).

The estrangement of the Seminoles from the network of social and political alliances that crisscrossed Creek country was completed during the separation phase, which Fairbanks (1978:171) considers to have occurred during the years 1763–1790. This phase coincides with the period of British rule in Florida. As the Seminoles anchored themselves within the tide of newly established trade networks along the St. Johns River, inland at Alachua and on the Suwannee, and at St. Marks in the panhandle, the archaeological visibility of their sites is marked by quantities of European-derived trade goods. Diplomatic and trade relations with the British colonial government in St. Augustine fostered the separation of Creek and Seminole. It is doubtful that the powerful Creek leader Alexander McGillivray had any real contact with the peninsular Seminoles during this period (Swan in Schoolcraft 1851–1857:vol. 5:260). The term "Seminole" or forms thereof appears with some regularity in colonial documents, on occasion with pejorative connotations.[9]

The development of an autonomous Seminole polity was evidently not accompanied by a process of political centralization. According to Fairbanks, squareground construction had been completely abandoned, and core elements of Seminole society, religion, and politics were undergoing simplification. Brushed pottery continued to be produced by Seminole women, often in the traditional jar and bowl forms typical of Creek ceramics.

In 1790–1840 a series of historical circumstances acted to diminish the organizational complexity of Seminole society further. Just prior to the resistance and removal phase (Fairbanks 1978:178), Florida was retroceded to Spain, which held it until 1821. In that year, Florida became a territory of the United States. With American propriety came the policies of Indian containment and removal. Through the implementation of four treaties during the years 1823–1833,[10] the Seminoles were effectively removed from their Florida lands and placed in the newly created Indian Territory on lands west of the Mississippi. The resistance on the part of some Seminoles is known to history as the Second Seminole War (1835–1842). Florida's living Seminoles are the descendants of those individuals who were not deported or killed outright during these seven years of hostilities.

The prosperity enjoyed by the Seminoles under British and Spanish rule vanished in the face of these events. The exchange of goods and products between Indian and white was interrupted and finally extinguished. The remaining Seminoles became increasingly isolated in "diffuse groups of farm homesteads" (Fairbanks 1978:184). Elements of native religion and politics underwent further simplification and decline. Ar-

chaeological correlates of this phase include sites with low artifact density and few trade goods present.

After 1840 the remaining Seminole resisters sought refuge
deep in the isolation of the southern Florida wetlands. Here,
during the withdrawal phase (1840–1880) they forged a new cultural identity based on their adaptations to subtropical conditions. Matrilocal pole and thatch "chickee" camps scattered in
the Everglades and Big Cypress swamps became the centers of
Seminole life, while an ethos of separation from American society prevailed (Fairbanks 1978:187, 188). The final phase covers
the last one hundred years of Seminole culture history. During
this time the Seminoles have experienced a crystallization of cultural adaptations to southern Florida environments and, in this
century, have adjusted to reservation life.[11]

The works of Charles Fairbanks were extremely influential in
forming conventional understandings of Seminole ethnohistory.[12] However, it is perhaps time to make a critical appraisal of
Fairbanks's contributions. His failure to offer any sustained consideration of the prehistoric foundations of historic Seminole society is particularly striking. The Seminole culture history
reconstructed by Fairbanks chronicles the political relations between Euro-Americans and Indians. The cultural transformations brought about by the Seminoles themselves receive little
attention. The reader of Fairbanks forms an impression of Seminole culture as that of a society unable to direct its own destiny
on the colonial frontier. This view is not surprising, given the initial scope of Fairbanks's Indian Claims work. Stimuli for culture
change developed from external pressures—environmental
challenges and Euro-American political domination.

The work of Craig and Peebles (1974) amplifies this theme.
Seminole culture is here defined in terms of its "remarkable ability to accomplish a swift succession of ethnoecologic changes"
(Craig and Peebles 1974:83). In the logic of biological analogy,
these changes were seen to occur as Seminole populations radiated into a variety of ecological niches. The authors suggest
that the Seminoles experienced four distinct ethnoecological
shifts between 1740 and 1840. The development of a unique
Seminole ethnicity correlates with these shifts.

The first change resulted from the adoption of pastoralism by the Seminoles. Reliance upon stock raising—cattle, hogs, and horses—increased through time as the skins and other products of these animals supplanted deerskins in the Florida trade.

Following American control of Florida, the skin trade dissolved, and the Indians were forced into a subsistence economy based on gardening. After 1818, faced with the reality of determined American aggression, the Seminoles sought remote locations in which to settle. The Gulf coast wetlands were ideal for this purpose but presented the Seminoles with an unfamiliar environment. However, the vegetable diet produced in family garden plots was successfully supplemented by shellfish, fish, and other food items obtained through hunting and gathering.

Between 1818 and 1850 settlements were temporary and shifting. Native religion, politics, and social organization were weakly developed. Finally, the survivors of the Second Seminole War effected the final shift by their adaptation to the subtropics of southern Florida, where their unique culture exists to this day.

The Craig and Peebles culture history presents a stress model of culture change. To the question "why were these Indians able to change their ethnoecology so often when other tribes failed?" (Craig and Peebles 1974:91), it is answered that they were simply forced to do so by the threat of cultural extinction. The authors had difficulty reconciling the presumed flexible nature of Seminole culture with the observed conservatism of its members (Craig and Peebles 1974:88). One possible explanation is that the capacity for change was introduced from outside. The authors suggest that the agents of change were the runaway blacks from the coastal plantations of the Carolinas and Georgia. These individuals brought with them a packet of survival skills honed in the coastal wetlands plus knowledge of American- and European-derived technology gained through laboring on the plantations. The blacks became indispensable to the Seminoles, who developed their own form of peculiar institution with the black Floridians.[13] To Craig and Peebles, Seminole society was steadfast in its ability to survive but was virtually devoid of complexity and richness.

William Sturtevant (1971) is the strongest advocate of the anthropological approach to Seminole culture history. In his view, Seminole culture history can be evaluated with respect to an aboriginal southeastern culture pattern. The strongest continuities are with core elements of historic Creek culture. Creek settlement patterning, religious and political institutions, and economic practices were all preserved in the Seminole culture of the eighteenth and early nineteenth centuries. The emergence of new forms of social organization represented transformations of previous configurations in which threads of cultural meaning were preserved. The defining mode of Seminole ethnicity, in Sturtevant's view, is the development of the busk group in the mid-1800s. Busk group members shared common sacra stored in a communal medicine bundle, which was entrusted to the care of a medicine man. The ritual and communal bonds experienced in the busk group were not unlike the bonds that existed in the traditional Creek *talwa*, or community. Aspects of southeastern Indian cosmology were thus kept alive through the practices of the busk group. According to Sturtevant, the referent for ethnicity is cultural, not environmental or political.

Previous interpretations of Seminole culture history are enormously useful in determining the broad historical context in which Seminole culture developed. Political circumstances have been, and will continue to be, important considerations in the study of Indians of the historic period. Cultural adaptations to environmental factors often have great impact on the development of cultures through time. Yet these considerations alone are not sufficient for understanding the evolution of Florida Seminole culture and history.

Antecedents
The Ancestral Creek Pattern

In order to develop a history of the Florida Seminoles independent of Euro-American documentation, one must review the
findings of prehistoric archaeology. This information is useful in
identifying the prehistoric foundations of the historic Creek culture from which the Seminoles derived.

Prehistoric Foundations

The historic Seminoles of Florida are undeniably descended
from tribes of Creek Indians and related groups who were encountered early in the historic period living in central Georgia,
in the Chattahoochee River drainage at the border of Georgia
and Alabama, and in the Coosa-Tallapoosa River drainages of
central Alabama (Swanton 1922). These Indians shared a similar
culture pattern and spoke languages of the Muskogean family.
Colonial authorities came to refer to the Indians of Georgia and
the Chattahoochee as Lower Creeks, while the Coosa-Tallapoosa bands were called Upper Creeks. The often volatile, always complex, and at times fickle political relationships
between these Indians and the French, Spanish, British, and
American authorities militates against easy generality, but contemporary accounts (Swan in Schoolcraft 1851–1857:vol. 5:278)

do suggest that the Upper and Lower Creeks were often divided with respect to allegiance.

It is not possible, given the present state of knowledge, to link known tribes of Upper or Lower Creeks with specific prehistoric archaeological assemblages. It is reasonable in some cases to postulate that there were in situ developments of the historic tribes in their respective areas. The historic Creeks are linked to prehistoric archaeological cultures by means of the Lamar ceramic series. The Lamar series, in prehistoric contexts, includes incised styles of vessel decoration that are held to be ancestral to historic Creek incised wares. The origins of the typical brushed pottery of the Creeks and Seminoles are more adequately demonstrated in the Upper Creek area than along the Chattahoochee. In the Coosa-Tallapoosa drainage, brushed pottery appears ca. A.D. 900–1000 and is associated with assemblages containing Creek-like notched and fluted rim styles (Dickens 1979:148). Brushed pottery comes to dominate the Chattahoochee assemblages from the mid-1700s onward (Schnell 1970; DeJarnette 1975:109,185), although its development here is not clear. However, prehistoric assemblages in the Lower Creek area also contain complicated stamped and check-stamped ceramics. These decorative techniques are absent in known historic Creek pottery (H. Smith 1948; Sears 1955; Fairbanks 1956:15; Wauchope 1966; Dickens 1979:147) but are present in Cherokee ceramics in north Georgia, Tennessee, and North Carolina (Lewis and Kneberg 1946; Caldwell 1955; Sears 1955). Cultural and historical factors in the development of historic Creek pottery thus remain to be worked out.

Other lines of evidence can be developed to demonstrate the connection between the historic Creeks and archaeological cultures of the lower Southeast. Scholars have suggested that the temple-mound culture of the late prehistoric Mississippian societies should be interpreted in light of described busk practices of the historic Creeks (Swanton 1928c; Willoughby 1932; Waring 1968). The annual busk and other ritual behaviors of the historic period are held to represent the historical transformation of Mississippian religion, which was organized into three complementary cults (Brown 1985; Knight 1986). Each of the cults served the

interests of different sectors of the community but also func-
tioned to integrate plural interests in these complex chiefdom-
level societies. The cults ensured proper relations with lineage
and clan ancestors, provided acceptable means for achieving
and marking status, affirmed core concepts about the Indian
cosmos and an individual's place in society, and served other
functions as well. While the cults and their meaning in the religious pantheon of the southeastern Indians were reconstituted
through time, aboriginal cultures in the Southeast appear also to
have been marked by remarkably persistent values attached to
what have been termed the "core metaphors" (Knight 1986).
The primary axes along which southeastern aboriginal beliefs
were ordered included dichotomies of balance and unbalance
and of purity and impurity. Thus the ritual preparation of the
Mississippian temple mounds by the application of earth man-
tles of clean white sand (Knight 1981) had its historical correlate
in the Seminole busk practice of adding a layer of clean white
sand to the dance circle.

Mississippian Survivals Among the Seminoles

The European presence in the sixteenth-century Southeast
was a catalyst for many changes in aboriginal society (M. Smith
1987). The changes that occurred included transformations in
the structure and meaning of the religious cults that together
comprised Mississippian religion. In the wake of widespread
population decline and dispersal due to European contact, cult
practices and sacra once associated with chiefly sectors became
more communal in nature (Knight 1986:682). Whereas mound
building in Mississippian societies is presumed to have had a
political function in the maintenance of the chiefly office, the ritual preparation of the busk ground in historic times had little to
do with politics but much to do with community solidarity. Core
beliefs were not abandoned but instead became the province of
a different sector of society. There is no reason to believe that
Mississippian religion was static until the coming of the Europeans. The historic transformation in aboriginal religion must

have had a precedent in prehistoric processes, despite the difficulties in discerning these processes in the archaeological record. It is reasonable to suppose that the Seminoles were cultural
heirs to a religious flexibility with roots deeper than the historical circumstances of European contact. In religious or cosmological terms, the Seminoles can be connected to the mainstream of
Mississippian culture; relatively little attention needs to be paid
to the contact experience.

One of the Mississippian religious cults is known as the warrior cult (Brown 1985) or the more broadly defined warfare/cos-
mogony complex (Knight 1986). The associated symbolism of
this cult includes representations of arrowheads, maces, and
other equipment of war; depictions of warriors dressed in ceremonial regalia; and composite beings with both human and animal features. This cult is thought to have glorified the deeds of
war and also to have provided a medium for the display of priest-
ly knowledge and ritual. The cult provided the social sanction
for the acquisition of status by priests and warriors.

The ethos imbued by the Mississippian warriors was to form
an integral part of the historic Seminole world view. In historic
times bravery was still marked by the ability of the warrior to
"bring in the hair" (Swan in Schoolcraft 1851–1857:vol. 5:280), a
practice which the Mississippian "trophy head" depictions presumably record (Willoughby 1932:54; Waring and Holder
1945:20). Scalping remained a common practice among Seminole warriors during the years of the Second Seminole War,
much to the horror of American citizens and the military
(Rowles 1841; Welch 1977).

Success at warring was determined by an individual's ability
to travel far from home, often in hostile and unknown territory,
to provision himself for an extended and uncertain journey, to
find the enemy target—often another war party or encampment—and to strike it successfully and return home with scalps
and other trophies of victory. Manhood was demonstrated
through tests of courage, skill, and ingenuity. These virtues
must be exhibited repeatedly throughout a person's life and
were necessary for success in the European deerskin trade,
which became a pervasive influence on the southeastern frontier

before the turn of the eighteenth century. European traders
found Indians eager to establish avenues of exchange with
them, not because of some Indian predilection for European
baubles, but because European mercantilism complemented already existing systems of aboriginal status and prestige (Waselkov and Paul 1981; Miller and Hamell 1986). In the context of
the European presence, successful warriors became successful
entrepreneurs, providing as evidence of their success not human trophies but the skins of beasts and taking as their reward
not beads of shell and stone but objects of glass, cloth, and
brass.

The composite beings of the prehistoric warfare/cosmogony
complex also had their counterparts in historic Seminole culture.
Reports from the 1800s describe the Seminole belief in a "monster, with a large serpent's body shining like silver, whose
breath is destructive to all who approach" (Pierce 1825:135).
Similar creatures appear in Mississippian cult motifs (Waring
and Holder 1945:16). The scales and/or horn of this or a similar
being are contained in the medicine bundles of the contemporary Seminoles and are held to have magical properties. The
bundles themselves figure importantly in the communal ritual
of the Seminoles and are featured at the annual Green Corn
Dance. Here they are carefully unwrapped by the Seminole
medicine man, inspected, and displayed during the Court Day
rites and during the concluding festivities. The bundle is under
the care of a religious specialist, but its objects are invested with
the power of community health and well-being. Mississippian
monsters have thus become very much the province of the common man.

The relationship between the Green Corn Dance of the historic Seminoles and platform mound rituals of Mississippian societies (Swanton 1928c; Willoughby 1932; Waring 1968; Howard
1968; Knight 1981, 1986) has been sufficiently indicated. Previous research has established the conceptual and physical links
between the prehistoric mound-building practices and historic
Creek busk ceremonialism, to which the Seminole Green Corn
Dance is closely related. Central to the Creek busk were rituals
concerned with purity, order, and fertility. The area in which

the rites were held was sanctified by the addition of a blanket of clean earth, on which a new fire was kindled (Adair 1986:106; Swanton 1932:177; Swan in Schoolcraft 1851–1857: vol. 5:268), and ears of ripening corn were brought for display. It has been suggested (Knight 1981, 1986) that these rites expressed the desire for human-induced order to prevail over the disorder of the natural world. Mississippian mound building reflected this metaphor writ large.[1]

It is also suggested that mound-building practices and busk ceremonialism were fundamental expressions of the Indians' desire to achieve a state of spiritual purity. The black drink ceremonies of the southeastern Indians have been cited as primary means through which purity could be attained. The ethnohistorical literature is replete with instances of the use of the black drinks among Muskogean peoples on political and ritual occasions (Adair 1986:25, 49, 114; Gatschet 1884:177–183; Swan in Schoolcraft 1851–1857:vol. 5:265–268; Hawkins 1980:318, 322; Payne 1985:180; Young 1934–1935:90; Rowles 1841; MacCauley 1887:522).[2]

Among the Seminoles of this century, the Green Corn Dance provided the principal opportunity for partaking in the black drinks. During the course of this event, men would imbibe a series of the herbal teas, each brewed from plants carefully selected for their presumed curative and purifying properties (Capron 1953:202; Sturtevant 1954:52–55).

Purification could be achieved in ways other than by drinking the black drink teas. Tobacco smoking and "scratching" or scarification also figured importantly in rites of purity. While the antiquity of these practices is not easy to establish, it is evident from documentary sources that smoking and scratching were often associated with the black drink ritual. Scratching among contemporary Seminoles is graphically recorded by Capron on the final day of the Green Corn ceremony:

> The scratching [with a scratcher constructed of six sewing needles mounted in a block of wood] consists of two long strokes on the front and two on the back of each upper arm and each lower arm; two front and two back on the thighs and two each on the lower

leg; two diagonal strokes on each breast and two diagonal strokes on each side of the back. . . . its purpose is to purify the blood and prevent blood poison. [Capron 1953:206–207][3]

All Seminole males, including infants, are scratched sometime during the ceremony. Smoking also figures in the Green Corn ritual, as again recorded by Capron:

In the meantime [after the men have taken a sweatbath] the Medicine Man has taken a little red cloth package from the Medicine Bundle and from this has taken a little pipe. He lights this and stands, facing the east and smoking it. He stands thus for a few moments, smoking, and then he sits down behind the Medicine Man's fire, facing west, and smokes for a few minutes more. Then he puts up the pipe and turns to the Medicine Bundle. [Capron 1953:207]

In this manner the Medicine Man prepares himself to unwrap the other objects in the bundle. If the object of this smoking was to free the Medicine Man of impurities and sanctify the atmosphere for the important events at hand, then the relationship to the calumet or "pipe of peace" ceremonies of the Indians of the Eastern Woodlands is clear. To judge from the archaeological recovery of smoking pipes from prehistoric sites in the East, smoking had long held some special but undetermined significance in aboriginal societies.[4]

Mississippian serpent motifs also appear in historic Seminole culture. Mississippian serpents, often resembling the rattlesnake, are included in a number of contexts that suggest their association with related beliefs about death and plant fertility (Brown 1985:126–127; Prentice 1986:263). Seminole beliefs appear to have emphasized the awesome and somewhat malevolent power of the rattlesnake itself (Bartram 1955:218–220; Capron 1956:71) and with the related panther motif of the Mississippian fertility pantheon took on specific, demystified meanings at the hands of the Seminoles.[5] Again, this process may relate to the historical transformation of the Mississippian cults following European contact and the decline in the power of aboriginal chiefdoms. The formation of the totemic clans of the contemporary Seminoles—Panther, Bird, Snake, and Deer—may have been taking place at about this time as lineages appropriated animals and their associated symbolism from the religious pantheon and developed group identities around them. It is admittedly difficult to correlate the known Seminole clans with totemic representations of panthers, birds, deer, or snakes, although it is notable that diamondback motifs appear with some frequency in Seminole beadwork (Goggin 1951:2–17; Piper and Piper 1982:223).

Although European contact had the consequences for the nature of aboriginal religion in the Southeast that I have noted, the relative immunity of the core elements of the Indian cosmos to the vicissitudes of history is more striking. The Seminole cosmos was, in form and in spirit, the legacy of the Mississippian cosmos. Even the recent successes of Christianity among the Seminoles constituted success in Indian terms (Buswell 1972). The four-part world of the Mississippians, symbolized by the circle-and-cross motif, was quite literally given embodiment by the Seminoles, as the following passage demonstrates in its discussion of the Seminole theory of disease:

> The spirit goes up north and likes it there. One spirit goes north and around to the east. Get east then go over Milky Way to the west and city of the dead. Then person die. In four days other ghost goes at night fall.
>
> At night sometimes one ghost goes north—likes it there but comes back before dawn. Person all right since dream. If goes north and a little way east, somebody sick, body shakes. Medicine man sing, call ghost back. Blow on pipes and go after ghost, bring it back to east, then south to middle. Get ghost back, person get well. [Greenlee 1944:319]

The cultural relationship between the Seminoles and southeastern aboriginal tradition is unequivocal and enduring (figures 2 and 3).In some instances, direct Mississippian iconography is discernible in vestigial form among the Seminoles of the ethnographic present. The survival among the Seminoles of core cosmological precepts of at least Mississippian-era antiquity suggests that anthropological views of the Seminoles as curious

Figure 2. The Seminoles as southeastern Indians: top, reconstructed prehistoric headdress from the Mississippian site of Cemochechobee; bottom, the Long Warrior's headdress in 1774. *Source:* After Schnell et al. 1981 and Bartram 1955.

tropical oddities or as mere addenda to the cultural evolution of aboriginal societies in the Southeast lack a necessary historical dimension. Instead it can be argued that the Seminoles are in fact quintessential southeastern Indians. Ethnohistory and archaeology can be combined to provide the conceptual framework for this argument under the rubric of the ancestral Creek pattern. In the ancestral Creek pattern the most direct cultural-

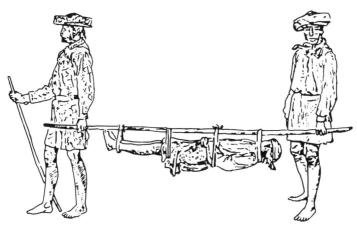

Figure 3. The Seminoles as southeastern Indians: top, a Natchez Indian burial in 1725; bottom, a Seminole burial in the 1870s. *Source:* After Hudson 1976 and after MacCauley 1887.

historical connections are expressed between the Seminoles and their southeastern heritage.

The Ancestral Creek Pattern

Just over one hundred years ago, at the request of the U.S. government, the Reverend Clay MacCauley visited the reservations of the southern Florida Seminoles. His landmark report, published in 1887, remarked concerning the Seminoles and their society: "so strong has the Creek influence been in their development that the Creek language, Creek customs, and Creek regulations have been the guiding forces in their history" (MacCauley 1887:495). Of what Creek customs and regulations did MacCauley write, and how can they be implicated as guiding forces in Seminole culture history? Answers to these questions must reflect not only fact gathering but also estimations of the processes of social and cultural change experienced by the late prehistoric and early historic Indians of the Southeast. Again, such considerations must begin with an examination of Mississippian societies.

Summary treatments of Mississippian societies (Wenke 1980:684; Fagan 1986:305) often convey the enduring but essentially incorrect view that at the time of initial European contact in the mid-sixteenth century Mississippian societies were highly complex, strongly hierarchical chiefdoms whose "collapse" can be attributed to the introduction of European diseases and a variety of contact-related phenomena. Despite archaeological indications that European contact had very real consequences for the prehistoric populations of the Southeast (M. Smith 1987), the view purveyed above is a static depiction of Mississippian cultures with little basis in fact. While European contact did engender transformations in aboriginal society, it is not reasonable to suppose that this was the first and only circumstance in which changes in aboriginal society occurred. Interpretations based on archaeology indicate that Mississippian societies were not marked by political stability but in fact experienced cycles of centralization and decentralization, in response to factors that are poorly understood but clearly had nothing to do with the coming of the Europeans. Thus Mississippian societies were continually being reconstituted through time. The implication is that the elite, or chiefly, sector of society was fundamentally unstable, while the lifeways of the commoners were marked by their persistence. The prevailing sociological trend was toward local, and presumably clan-based, autonomy.

There are indications that chiefly authority across a broad area of the Southeast was weakened between about A.D. 1300 and A.D. 1500. Artifacts and motifs associated with the Mississippian ancestor cults, probably under the control of priests but conducted through the auspices of the chief, decline in frequency between these years, while iconography associated with communal fertility (Green Corn) ritual is on the rise (Brown 1985:102). Settlement pattern data also hint at the process of political instability that was now taking place.

At the Shoulderbone site in the Oconee valley of central Georgia archaeological excavations indicate that this multiple mound center was abandoned sometime during the fifteenth century (Williams and Shapiro 1986). Meanwhile, in the Coosa River drainage of central Alabama, the aboriginal polities that the sixteenth-century Spanish conquistadores would encounter were just now forming (Hudson et al. 1985). Chiefdoms in the Florida panhandle were experiencing similar cycles of rise and decline (Scarry 1984).

The archaeological sequence at the site of Tukabatchee on the Tallapoosa River in central Alabama illustrates particularly well the final trend of sociopolitical decentralization that characterized the transition from the prehistoric to historic periods in the Southeast. Late prehistoric Mississippian societies at Tukabatchee were organized into a chiefdom settled in a nucleated village around a central platform mound (Knight 1985:53). Chiefs, or priest-chiefs, managed an agrarian, redistributive economy and as their reward took prestige items of imported shell and copper (Knight 1985:173). By A.D. 1600 the chiefdom at Tukabatchee had dissolved; ceremonies ceased to be performed atop the platform mound, and it fell into disuse. Imported objects of shell and copper were no longer the primary markers of status but were largely replaced by a flood of trade items obtained from European missionaries, merchants, and diplomats (Knight 1985:174–176, 179). These items have been recovered in the household refuse of the Tukabatchee villagers, and so it can be inferred that wealth was no longer confined to the chiefly sector of society.

With the coming of the European-inspired deerskin trade in the late 1600s, greater emphasis fell on the individual as the unit of production, distribution, and consumption, and the office of chief was further undermined. The form of social organization that correlated with the economic emphasis on the individual was the extended family household compound. At Tukabatchee, these domestic compounds were located some 200 m from one another and consisted of two to four buildings surrounding a central courtyard or square (Knight 1985:118).

Colonial documents from this period often refer to the Indian leaders as chiefs (or, occasionally, "kings"; see Hawkins 1980:317, for one example), but it is clear from these documents and the combined archaeological evidence that these individuals shared little in common with the chiefs of the Mississippian polities. Their function as agents of economic redistribution was greatly reduced by the atmosphere of individual autonomy promoted by the deerskin entrepreneurs. The sacred connotations of the office virtually vanished with the disappearance of the ancestor cults. However, conditions along the colonial frontier were right for the development of a new breed of Indian leader. These men were adept at reading the hidden agendas of Indian and European policies with regard to the vital concerns of the colonial frontier—land cessions and trade regulations. Thus the Creek Confederacy emerged at the hands of these men and attempted to present a united Indian front in the face of European trading irregularities and territorial expansion. The demands of a united policy at times required the leaders of the Confederacy to quash dissension from local chiefs forcibly (Swan in Schoolcraft 1851–1857:vol. 5:281), and the picture is often one of duplicity and subterfuge (Doster 1967). The success of Indian leadership depended to a large extent on the ability to unveil the cloaked intentions of the French, British, and Spanish colonial governments, weigh the advantages or disadvantages of compliance or resistance to the goals of the colonists, and judge the support that the leader was likely to receive once his response had been determined. Support from other Indians was neither steadfast or guaranteed, and the social reality was one of near-constant fissioning and realignment in the population.

Briefly restated, the major trends in the social transition between the late prehistoric and historic periods in the interior Southeast are as follows:

- transformations in the structure of religious cult institutions, but a persistence among historic Indians of the basic prehistoric cosmology
- the cyclical rise and decline of chiefdom-level sociopolitical authority
- a decentralization of chiefdom level organization in the early historic period, accompanied by an emphasis on local (clan?) and ultimately individual autonomy

In the historic period, these additional trends become evident:

- the Indian behaviors that permit the success of the deerskin trade are based on indigenous systems of male prestige reckoning that date to late prehistoric times, if not before
- Euro-Indian colonial diplomacy accelerated the further development of Indian factionalism but also promoted some interest in pan-tribal sociopolitical organization. Acculturation proceeded in two distinct social realms—between Indian tribes or bands and between Indian and colonist.[6]

The consequences of these processes for the development of the Florida Seminoles are integral factors in the determination of the culture history of that people. The Seminoles were heirs not only to the basic southeastern aboriginal culture pattern but also to the historical process through which that pattern was preserved and transformed through time. Before these concerns can be properly evaluated, some consideration must be given to the founding stock of traits from which Seminole culture developed. I term these traits, together with their social and processual contexts, the ancestral Creek pattern.

Social Organization

The fundamental unit of interaction in Creek society was the nuclear family. The nuclear family was also the minimal unit of residence. Related women and their families maintained households close together, in effect forming small matrilineal communities. These communities are called *huti* (Swanton 1928b:171). It is clear from this informant's description that the term *huti* refers not only to the physical setting of the household but also to an implied set of economic responsibilities and obligations. Therefore, a woman's huti was in fact her home, while a man's huti was not his residence but the home of his mother and other matriclan members. The following description applies to the huti arrangement as it existed among the Upper Creeks in the late 1700s: "These houses stood in clusters of four, five, six, seven, and eight together, irregularly distributed up and down the banks of rivers or small streams; each cluster of houses contains a clan, or family of relations, who eat and live in common" (Swan in Schoolcraft 1851–1857:vol. 5:262).

To "eat and live in common" suggests that important domestic tasks were shared by female members of the huti. These tasks probably included plant cultivation; the crafts of weaving, pottery, and basketry; and raising children. The clusters of houses were probably arranged into domestic squaregrounds, as recounted in the following passage by the famed naturalist William Bartram, in which he describes his visit to the site of Coolome on the Tallapoosa River: "Every habitation consists of four oblong square houses, of one story, of the same form and dimension, and so situated as to form an exact square, encompassing an area of about a quarter of an acre of ground, leaving an entrance into it at each corner" (Bartram 1955:318). The excavation of a similar compound at Tukabatchee produced artifact patterns to suggest that each of the buildings was used for special purposes and may have housed male and female activities (Knight 1985:109, 117, 118).

Each huti was affiliated with a squareground town, where the town chief, or *mico*, resided. This larger community was known as the talwa, and its members were regarded as "people of one fire" (Swanton 1928b:246), in obvious reference to the sacred fire of the busk ceremony. Thus the talwa was the shared unit of political allegiance and community ritual. Talwa leadership was divided between the offices of mico; his advisers, or *henihas*; and the *tastanagi*, or war chief. During the busk or at town councils, these men occupied different cabins in the squareground, according to their office. In the typical arrangement, the mico and henihas sat in the western cabin, facing east. The tastanagi and warriors sat to the south, facing north, while the buildings on the east and north were occupied by visitors and other males of the talwa.

Clan affiliation was an important organizational principle in Creek society. This often took on tangible expression, as in the huti arrangement of the matriclan. Creek clans were further organized into moieties, classified on the basis of the red-white color opposition that was fundamental to Creek thought. Tastanagis were invariably selected from red clans according to the reasoning that red was the color of war, while white clans supplied the mico and henihas.[7] Talwas were also classified as red or white and were pitted against one another in the famous ball game of the southeastern Indians, known to them as the "brother of war" (Swanton 1928b:459).

In Creek life, too, a strong distinction was made between male and female activities. Oral traditions of this century preserve the fundamental and pervasive nature of this distinction, as evidenced in the statement that "in ancient times men and women were almost like two distinct peoples" (Swanton 1928b:384). The role of women in the domestic economy was described in various ways by the eighteenth-century chroniclers. While one account indicated that "every domestic drudgery [is] imposed upon their women" (Pope 1979:60–62), another viewed the women as "industrious, frugal, [and] careful" (Bartram 1955:385). Women were rewarded for their industry with the

love and esteem of their husbands, who undoubtedly understood and appreciated the contributions of their wives to the
maintenance of the household. As a result, American efforts in
the early 1800s to provide home industries for the women,
thereby granting them some measure of autonomy, were stoutly
opposed by Indian men (Hawkins 1980:354).

The combined documentary testimony leaves little doubt that
the worlds of Indian men and women were indeed very different. While the woman's place was the huti, the man's place was
on the warpath or hunting trail. Creek hunters traveled the Florida peninsula as far south as the Everglades in search of game.[8]
Their main prey was the white-tailed deer. Warfare and deer
hunting may have been communal events, requiring the absence of most of the males from any particular village for an extended length of time. However, the object of Creek warfare
was not conquest but the individual taking of scalps to demonstrate a warrior's prowess and courage. A first-time warrior successful in obtaining an enemy scalp earned the right to be called
a "man and a warrior" and was honored with a war name (Swan
in Schoolcraft 1851–1857:vol. 5:280). Prestige would accrue with
the accumulation of scalps, and a warrior could thus climb the
ranks of authority and veneration.

Such was the social legacy that the Creeks passed on to the
Seminoles. The fundamental social relations—the family, the
huti, and the clan—were tenaciously preserved by the Seminoles throughout their cultural development in Florida. However, there is little indication that the Florida Seminoles ever
considered themselves subject to the policies of the Creek Confederacy, and Confederacy leader Alexander McGillivray seldom if ever had any real contact with these southern bands
(Swan in Schoolcraft 1851–1857:vol. 5:260). The Cowkeeper,
headman of the Alachua band of Seminoles, was one individual
who kept himself purposely aloof from Confederacy affairs and
preferred to deal with colonial authorities on his own terms
(Covington 1961:39). Thus in one estimation (Swan in Schoolcraft 1851–1857:vol. 5:263), the Seminoles were wont to act in-
dependently of the interests of other Indians.

The processes that accompanied the social transformation

from Creek to Seminole most strongly affected the moiety relations between clans and the sets of ritual obligations that bound
together various towns. The Florida frontier felt the menacing
effects of roving bands of rogue Indians whose plunderous activities produced the "Indian troubles" of the colonists. Had the
moiety system been intact, these men would have been bound
in a web of sanctioned behaviors—warring, scalping, the ball
play—that would have provided means for obtaining status in
traditionally recognized ways. By comparison with the Creeks,
the Seminoles seem to have exhibited little coercive social order
of the sort that was necessary to keep individuals in line, with
the result that a number of pejorative comments were made
about these Indians, including the following from Swan (in
Schoolcraft 1851–1857:vol. 5:260): "They are considerably numerous, but poor and miserable beyond description; being so
thinly scattered over a barren desert, they seldom assemble to
take black drink, or deliberate on public matters, like the upper
and lower Creeks," or, and more to the point, "their country is
a place of refuge for vagrants and murderers from every part of
the nation, who, by flying from the upper and lower districts to
this desert, are able to elude the pursuit and revenge of even the
Indians themselves." Swan's narration then turns to an account
of a prominent Seminole named Kinnard who resided near the
confluence of the Flint and Chattahoochee rivers. This man, said
by Swan to be one of the leaders of the Seminoles and a "noted
trader, farmer, and herdsman," was principally renowned for
shooting his Negroes as he pleased and for cutting off the ears
of one of his wives in a drunken frenzy.

While most Seminoles were not cast in the mold of Kinnard
(indeed, Bartram [1955:200] was impressed by the "lofty and
majestic countenance" of the White King of the Talahoschte
Seminoles), there were clear reasons why individuals in Seminole society would act with increasing self-assurance and with
less regard for the traditional norms of the social hierarchy.
Much of this attitude had to do with the climate of free enterprise that pervaded colonial relations in Florida, an atmosphere
in which the developing Seminole ethnicity was to thrive.

Economy and Subsistence

Conventional views of Seminole culture history have stressed the roles of the environment and changing subsistence practices in bringing about the genesis of Seminole ethnicity. In one estimation (Craig and Peebles 1974) the coastal and freshwater wetlands of Florida confronted the Seminoles with adaptive challenges not previously experienced in their Creek piedmont homeland, while in another opinion (Fairbanks 1978), the new adaptive challenge was provided in the form of cattle pastoralism on the vast interior Florida savannas. The net social effect of these processes of cultural adaptation was the simplification of Seminole society, politics, and religion.

These views have attempted to explain the dispersed, non-centralized settlement pattern and associated lifeways that came to characterize Florida Seminole life. With reference to the ancestral creek pattern, these approaches can be critiqued on a number of grounds. First, there is every reason to believe, on the basis of archaeology and ethnohistory in the Creek area, that the nuclear family was an important and economically viable unit that occupied, for at least portions of the year, special-purpose campsites in relatively remote locations. Sites of this nature on the Apalachicola River levees of northern Florida have been dated by archaeologists (Brose 1980:20–22) to about A.D. 1300. In late prehistoric chiefdom-level societies of the interior Southeast, these nuclear families would have been bonded in a web of lineage-organized redistributive or obligatory relationships ultimately controlled by the chief (Muller 1987:20). Historic Creek sites dating to the eighteenth and early nineteenth centuries in the Chattahoochee River drainage (Schnell 1970; DeJarnette 1975) do not appear to have been densely nucleated settlements; instead they might have been locations where families or extended family groups resided in close enough proximity to form a village. Thus one might argue that the traditional cultural emphasis of the southeastern Indians had always been on the nuclear family or the matrilineal extended family—these were the fundamental units of economic and social relations that formed the lowest denominator of aboriginal lifeways. It is not unusual for the emphasis on family to persist among the Seminoles, because it was a strong element in Creek culture. But because the Seminoles were largely removed from the intrigues of the Creek Confederacy, chroniclers who recorded Seminole life remarked more upon its domestic aspects than upon the political ones.

Were Seminole lifeways dramatically different from customs and practices of the Creeks? While logic suggests that the wetland and savanna habitats of Florida would require new cultural strategies of adaptation, history and archaeology argue against the notion that Creek subsistence practices were restricted to piedmont farming and woodland hunting. Creek artifacts have been recovered from the famous Stallings Island site on the Savannah River in Georgia, with an indication that the site was used as a camp for procuring riverine resources (Fairbanks 1942:227). In the central Alabama piedmont, archaeology of Atasi Phase (A.D. 1600–1715) house sites has demonstrated that a wide variety of plant and animal species were used for food, including freshwater mollusks, species of turtle and fish, squirrel, raccoon, oppossum, deer, wild fruits, and hickory nuts (Knight 1985:78–81). While deer hunting may have provided the Indians with the greatest percentage of their meat consumption, a broad spectrum of resources contributed to the diet throughout the Upper Creek area (Waselkov 1985:79). There have been suggestions that the historic Creeks relied upon a greater variety of wild foods than had their prehistoric ancestors (Fairbanks 1962:55), and there are no signs that this trend was reversed in the nineteenth century (Knight 1985:151–153; Dickens 1979:171). Fishing appears to have acquired some importance for the Creeks, as its technology involved the use of fire-hardened spears, plant poisons for stunning fish (Swanton 1946:338, 341–343), and fishing with a hook and line. Several species of catfish and freshwater drum were taken by the Creeks of Taskigi town (Waselkov 1985:86). Brass fishhooks were included as burial goods at the Jackson site, a historic Creek village in the Chattahoochee Basin dating to the mid-1700s (DeJarnette 1975:115–130).

Colonial documents record the fact that the Creek Indians included all of the Florida peninsula in their hunting grounds, and therefore they are assumed to have been quite familiar with the available resources of the area in their extended forays into the more southern wetlands and hammocks. It is not unusual for the first Seminole settlements in the Florida colony to have been located around the prairie ponds and lakes of the interior or in the river drainages of the peninsula or panhandle. These areas offered resources with which the Seminoles, as Creeks, had already become acquainted. In addition, the vast interior savannas offered the colonial Seminoles another advantage—natural forage for herds of domesticated cattle.

Cattle have been regarded as playing an important role in promoting culture change among the first Seminoles, especially those associated with Cowkeeper's band that settled the Alachua savanna in the 1740s and began herding animals descended from introduced Spanish stock (Fairbanks 1978:169, 175). This view involves several assumptions. First, cattle herding itself is regarded as a dispersed activity that encourages a dispersal of social institutions. Nucleated village life is one of the first things to disappear. Second, cattle ownership is seen to promote the development of wealth differences between men, accelerating the process of social divisiveness that is already under way. This argument can be developed, because cattle were used by the Creeks and Seminoles to replace or supplement deer in the European skin trade, and the profits from this trade were accrued on an individual basis. Finally, because cattle husbandry was, like deer hunting, essentially a male activity, it provided yet another way for Indian males to acquire wealth and prestige and to maintain their social dominance over Indian women. While these assumptions are certainly not groundless, additional cultural and historical factors need to be considered before a more comprehensive evaluation of cattle pastoralism among the early Seminoles can be offered.

First there is the matter of history. The assumption that the Seminoles received their first exposure to cattle herding on the Alachua plain in the mid-eighteenth century is not supported by recent archaeology conducted in the Creek area. The Upper Creeks of central Alabama had, by 1730 and perhaps before, adopted the use of cattle, pigs, and chickens from the Europeans (Waselkov 1985:80), and by the middle decades of that century cattle ownership had become an important ingredient in the determination of prestige and in the inheritance of wealth (Fabel 1974:108). One man with the formidable name of "Bully," who resided in a squareground town on the lower Chattahoochee, was said to possess "tolerable industry" partly because he had amassed a cattle herd numbering more than five hundred head (Pope 1979:64).

Thus a cattle complex was well established among the Creeks and may have been introduced sometime before the Seminole settlement of the Florida peninsula. If one wishes to claim that the adoption of cattle herding among the Seminoles promoted social change, then similar or correlated changes should be evident among the Creeks. However, there is no clear evidence for the simplification of Creek society or politics during this time; in fact the trend may have been toward increasing complexity.

Other cross-cultural examples also suggest that the social consequences of a cattle-oriented economy may be quite different from those proposed for the Seminoles (Fairbanks 1978:169, 175). In the cattle belt of east Africa, men are actually tightly bonded into lineal groups whose "ordered anarchy" (Evans-Pritchard 1940:181) provides for decision making and the settlement of disputes. The primary unit of social life is the village, where the members of a number of different lineages reside. While village politics and religion are not centralized to any appreciable degree, there is every indication that cattle ownership engendered an intricate web of obligations and responsibilities through which all members of the community are drawn tightly together. The net effect is underlying solidarity, not the social fragmentation one might expect, given the fact that cattle are individually owned, are used to display wealth and prestige, and figure prominently in individually sponsored ritual.

Cattle pastoralism has no logical social consequences that exist apart from the historical and cultural contexts in which it is embedded along with other cultural practices and institutions.

No single or simple factors can explain the development of a unique Seminole ethnicity without reference to the specific historical and cultural circumstances in which these factors have evolved. I will now consider the combination of factors that influenced the cultural trajectory of the Florida Seminoles.

Colonization,
1716–1767

The first Creek bands to move permanently into the Florida wilderness in the early decades of the 1700s were probably well aware of the advantages of migration. Spanish envoys had been sent among them to tout the benefits of living in a Spanish colony (Boyd 1949; Goggin 1963:41; Fairbanks 1978) just at a time when frictions on the southeastern frontier between aboriginal factions and the European superpowers made living there particularly tenuous. By now many Creek Indians had become accustomed to the relative prosperity afforded by the deerskin trade and other ventures and had become increasingly disgruntled with the frequent depradations of whites and Indians in the interior Southeast. Between 1716 and 1767 the first major penetration of the Florida peninsula by those Indians soon to be dubbed "Seminoles," commonly translated as "wild ones," had been accomplished, and with them came the cultural complex that would give rise to the Seminole peoples of today.

It is not entirely correct to speak of the Florida Indians of this early period as Seminoles. The first recorded use of the term appears in field notes accompanying the surveyor DeBrahm's map of Florida in 1765 (Goggin 1963:53); his "Seminolskees" was used apparently as a generic term applied to any Indians he encountered in the peninsula during his mapping expedition for the colonial British government. The term "Seminole" appears with some regularity with reference to the Florida Indians in

travelers' accounts (Swan in Schoolcraft 1851–1857:vol. 5:260;
Bartram 1955:110, 206, 214) and colonial records of the second
Spanish administration in Florida (Zespedes to Galvez, August
16, 1784, in Lockey 1945:254). The Spanish derivation of the
term from "cimarrone," meaning "wild" or "runaway" (Sturtevant 1971:105; Fairbanks 1978:171)), suggests that it may have
been in limited use in the colony during the first Spanish period,
prior to 1763.

The term "proto-Seminole" has appeared in the ethnohistoric
literature in reference to the early bands of Creek migrants in
Florida. Although it is cumbersome, the term is well chosen.
Curiously, the term "Seminole" has come into common use
only of late among the Florida Indians themselves and for reasons of political expediency with respect to organizing and in-
corporating a legally designated tribe. Indians who did not wish
to join the Seminole Tribe, Inc., after its formation in 1957, later
organized the Miccosukee Tribe of Indians and were granted
federal reservation lands adjoining the Tamiami Trail, north of
Everglades National Park in present-day Dade County (see King
1978 for related discussion). While they speak the Mikasuki language, as do most Seminoles, they claim to have an independent tribal history from the Seminole Tribe (Sturtevant
1971:121).

The tribal identities and paths of migration of the early Seminole (Creek) bands were the subject of Fairbanks's detailed ethnohistorical report before the Indian Claims Commission
(Fairbanks 1974). This work stands as the definitive study of the
relationships between the Indian pioneers of Florida and the European colonial authorities and of the eventual coalescence by
1800 of the disparate bands into what Fairbanks termed
(1978:331) the "Seminole nation." However, as I noted earlier,
little attention was paid in this report (and perhaps not improp-
erly, given the terms of the contract) to Seminole Indian culture.
Little emphasis was placed on the roles of native beliefs, customs, and practices in influencing the development of Seminole
culture history. Until key colonial-period Seminole villages can
be located and excavated, for example the town of Alachua
(Latchaway) and the Lake Miccosukee settlements, the main

lines of cultural reconstruction must be developed from documentary sources. Two archaeological sites important to our discussion are the locations of Oven Hill (8Di15), on and in the Suwannee River, and A-296 (8Al296), on the eastern margin of Payne's Prairie east of present-day Gainesville. Important documents include the "humble petition" of the Englishman Denys Rolle, the journals and narratives of John and William Bartram, and records of the British Colonial Office. The combined data of archaeology and the historical record indicate remarkable continuity between the Seminoles and the ancestral Creek pattern but also suggest the beginnings of significant changes.

There is some indication that the vestiges of the old town moiety system were still extant with the very early Seminoles. In the Creek society "red" towns were pitted against "white" in the ball game, and the related activities of intertown raiding and warfare provided young men with the opportunity to prove their prowess and courage and to rise among the ranks of the warriors. In the unsettled conditions of the colonial frontier, mobile groups of men also found themselves in the best position to gain information about conditions in the world at large, information which was conveyed to the mico and other talwa members in the squareground upon their return. Raiding and the ball play along moiety lines were sanctioned activities by which men could accrue prestige, either through acts of bravery or simply by gathering useful information. The desire for prestige was so strong among southeastern aboriginal males that, should there be a breakdown in the sanctioned means for its achievement, we might expect alternative pathways to develop.

The implications of these processes for the nature of Euro-Indian relations in Florida can be illustrated with reference to the account of Denys Rolle (1977), a prospective colonial entrepreneur, who in 1764 set out from the St. Johns River near present Palatka on an overland journey to St. Marks (southeast of Tallahassee) to examine land granted him there by British colonial governor James Grant. Rolle passed through two Indian towns on his route west. The first he called Latchaway (Rolle 1977:48), presumably the "ancient Alachua town" of the later Bartram account (Bartram 1955:169); the second was on the west

bank of the "little Savannah" (Suwannee) River and was inhabited by the "Savannah Indians" (Rolle 1977:50, 52). These towns
appear to have been principal locations of the Seminole in the
north peninsula at that time.

After crossing the Suwannee, Rolle parlayed briefly with the
"White King" of the town but failed to meet with the headmen
at Latchaway because they were out on a hunt. On his return
trip, Rolle found that men of the Suwannee settlement had gone
to Latchaway, for "some diversion of the ball" (Rolle 1977:52).
This activity was directed by the White King. Rolle also remarked, in a rather judgmental tone, that the combined group
of Indians had consumed some eighteen casks of rum (as much
as eighteen hundred gallons but perhaps watered down) in less
than two weeks (Rolle 1977:52). Despite the suggestion that the
males of these two important Seminole towns were still linked
by means of ritual play and festivity, the Suwannee Seminoles
were led by their White King, not his red, or war clan, counterpart, as might be expected in traditional Creek society.

The clan moiety system within the towns was in the process
of collapse and perhaps in the case of the Suwannee Indians was
only in de facto existence. This disintegration released numbers
of prestige-hungry young men from the grip of social sanction,
and already on the Florida frontier there had appeared the troublesome "roving bands of Indians" (Goggin 1963:5) whose
transgressions of colonial law ranged from murder (Grant to
Board of Trade, August 5, 1766, in Grant 1772) to horse stealing,
plunder, and raiding (Bartram 1955:75, 214, 216).[1] In Bartram's
words, these "predatory bands" (Bartram 1955:214) were composed of young men of "singular elegance, richly ornamented
with silver plates, chains, and after the Seminole mode, with
waving plumes of feathers on their crests" (Bartram 1955:206).
Clearly, these young men were out to test their skills in the
world of opportunity provided by the colonial frontier. That
they no longer felt bound to the system created by clan or town
moieties is certain, and by the late 1760s we can assume that the
system was no longer meeting Indian needs of prestige
enhancement.

The process of moiety disintegration had been under way in

the Alachua area for some time when Bartram traveled to the Seminole settlements there in 1774. His accounts of the Cowkeeper and the Long Warrior provide us with an interesting analog, on the individual level, of what might be termed the red and white personalities that had developed by that time. The rather regal Cowkeeper, by birth an Oconee Creek and the founder of the Alachua band of Seminoles, was attended by Yamassee Indian slaves, who looked upon him with emotions of fear and esteem because, although "his eyes were lively and full of fire," "his countenance [was] manly and placid" (Bartram 1955:164). Cowkeeper's dress was simple and his deportment calm. He altogether conveyed the ideal image of a traditional Creek town chief, or mico.

The description in the documents of Long Warrior, Cowkeeper's associate or "second" (his red counterpart), offers a contrasting glimpse into Seminole behavior of the time. When the Long Warrior and his trading party of forty men were refused credit by the trader M'Latchee (as indeed M'Latchee was bound to do by colonial law), Long Warrior threatened the trader with a bolt of lightning sufficient to turn his store into "dust and ashes," demonstrating his reputed ability to commune with "powerful and invisible beings or spirits" (Bartram 1955:215). The ink sketch Bartram drew of Long Warrior (see the 1955 edition of his *Travels* on pages 184–185) and the graphic description he provided of the Seminole costume of the era further illustrate the social processes the Seminole were then experiencing. In an atmosphere of wildly fluctuating partisanship, on a frontier increasingly peopled with half-breeds and cunning entrepreneurs, the grand and gaudy Seminole costume (plumes, silver gorgets, and the like) immediately announced ethnic affiliation and marks of individual personality and achievement.

New trends in native leadership were indeed emerging as moiety bonds weakened, yet other aspects of the ancestral Creek pattern proved more enduring. The traditional talwa plan of settlement was transplanted in full by the migrant Creeks and was replicated by the Seminole across the Florida landscape. Rolle was entertained by the White King and the Suwannee Seminoles in a squaregroundlike area where they were seated upon "their couches of repose," taking the black drink as they do "when they have a mind to talk" (Rolle 1977:50).

When Bartram visited Cowkeeper's Cuscowilla, south of present-day Paynes Prairie near Micanopy, a public assembly took place there in the "public square or councilhouse" (Bartram 1955:167), where residents gathered from their domestic square-ground compounds, each of "two houses nearly the same size, about thirty feet in length, and about the same in height" (Bartram 1955:168). Likewise, the town of Talahoschte, founded by the White King and his followers on the east bank of the Su-wannee sometime after Rolle's visit, consisted of a square-ground where "the king, war chief, and several ancient chiefs and warriors were seated in royal cabins, the rest of the head-men and warriors, old and young, sat on cabins on the right hand [to the south] of the king's cabin's on the left, and on the same elevation are always assigned for white people, Indians of other towns, and such of their own people as choose" (Bartram 1955:200). Evidently the Talahoschte squareground consisted of three cabins around a central plaza. Seating for the king, war chief, and advisers faced east; other important males sat to the right and faced north, while visitors and others sat facing south.

A variation in squareground construction is presented by a Seminole village founded on the St. Johns River near the present city of Palatka between the years 1767–1774 that perhaps harked back to a time when southeastern squaregrounds were entirely roofed over (Waring 1968:55).[2] According to Bartram, at this place there was

> a grand, airy pavilion in the center of the village. It was four square; a range of pillars or posts on each side supporting a canopy composed of Palmetto leaves, woven or thatched together, which shaded a level platform in the center, that was ascended to from each side by two steps or flights, each almost twelve inches high, and seven or eight feet in breadth, all covered with carpets, curiously woven, of split canes dyed of various colors. [Bartram 1955:250, 251]

By 1774, the towns of Cuscowilla and Talahoschte and the Pal-

atka town were clearly the formal nuclei of sociopolitical integration. To the west, in the Chattahoochee valley and near the
site of Tallahassee, Jack Kinnard and the Bully were also well established in squareground towns. Important events were presented and arbitrated here as in the Creek towns, and there is
little indication that the so-called dispersed or diffuse settlement
pattern (Fairbanks 1978:175) had come to characterize Seminole
life.

Given the growing complexity of Euro-Indian relations to
which colonial documents attest, it is to be expected that the Indians would have maintained some formal means of processing
information in regular, socially meaningful ways. While the
Seminoles were increasingly aloof from the mandates of the
Creek confederacy, there is no indication of an overall weaken-
ing in their political organization at this time. Squaregrounds
continued to function among the peninsular and panhandle
Seminole bands as loci of sociopolitical integration (Fairbanks
1978:175 offers a different opinion).

Further indications that the talwa system persisted among the
Seminoles are the family homesteads and the matrilocal communities known in the Creek area as huti. Bartram (1955:163)
encountered three or four Indian habitations near a prehistoric
mound on his approach to Cuscowilla from the east, and just
north of the Alachua savanna he passed through another small
village containing four or five habitations. Its residents had left
their dwellings and well-stocked corncribs behind, and were encamped in what Bartram described as tents on a hunting trip by
the banks of a stream some miles to the north (Bartram 1955:180,
181). On the basis of Bartram's account, the Cuscowilla settlement pattern can be reconstructed to include the squareground
town itself, with thirty or more habitations and at least two outlying settlements, each containing up to five households.[3]

A Seminole Household

It is ironic that the town center of Cuscowilla has not yielded
to archaeological discovery, while the remains of its seemingly

less visible satellite communities have come to light (Mykel 1962). The site of A-296 (as designated in the State of Florida Master Site File in 1959) is of special interest because it may represent a portion of the hamlet noted by Bartram north of Cuscowilla on the northern margin of the savanna (Bartram 1955:180, 181). According to Bartram, the site was a sandy ridge, like the site of A-296 (Sears 1959:25; Mykel 1962). The "large creek of excellent water" (Bartram 1955:181) where its people were then camping was probably the Santa Fe River.

Sears's (1959) excavations at A-296 delimited a midden stain 6 m in diameter with six posthole features and recovered 679 sherds, 1 projectile point, 2 fragments of a trade pipestem, and several unidentifiable iron fragments. Most of the sherds are the type Chattahoochee Brushed, first defined by Bullen (1950) from collections along the Chattahoochee River in Florida and now assumed to be a cultural marker of the distribution and presence of Creek peoples throughout the Southeast. Rimsherds are plain and are notched or "angled" on the top of the rim. The notched rims bear a strong resemblance to sherds recovered by Goggin at the Indian trading house of Spalding's Lower Store (Lewis 1969), established on the St. Johns River in the early 1770s. Further similarities in the paste, or clay composition, of the sherds, as well as other attributes suggest strong affinities between the Seminole components of both sites.

The function of the building that once stood at the site has not been determined. Bartram's account mentioned that corncribs were standing in the hamlet, and they may have produced the posthole pattern noted by Sears. He suggested that the structure was temporary in nature, but a look at descriptions of other temporary buildings of the historic Seminoles (MacCauley 1887:502; Sturtevant 1962:77) indicates that fewer posts were used than are present at A-296.

Two important observations may be made with regard to the material culture of the site. First, trade goods are few in number. Second, lip and rim treatment on the pottery shows little variation. Trade activities, such as they were, centered in the square-grounds and were more the concern of people living there. Some trading did occur between the mobile "flying camps" of

Seminoles (Bartram 1955:110) and colonial traders, but it is not known whether such groups normally resided in the square-grounds or in hamlets. There may have been an increasing social distance between the more far-flung members of a Seminole talwa and the residents of its squareground, exacerbated by differences in wealth accumulation between the two groups, with the eventual outcome that the talwa system would split along these lines.

Pottery sherds recovered from A-296 indicate that seven to nine vessels were present at the site. At least one vessel was a bowl, and the others were jars. Jars had rims either lip notched or plain, while notching just below the lip appears only on the bowl. Both vessel forms included brushed and plain surface treatments. The limited repertoire of rim decoration suggested to Sears (1959:29) that rim styles of Seminole pottery may prove to correlate with some unit of cultural reality. It is possible that this unit is the huti, or the community formed by a group of related women. In this view, these women would manufacture pottery with a rim style (or styles) unique to their clan affiliation; pottery would be a decorative marker of clan membership. Thus we would not expect to find many different styles of rim decoration on sherds from the same Seminole site. The recovery of virtually identical lip-notched sherds from A-296 and Spalding's Lower Store and the rarity of this rim style at other Florida sites suggest that the two deposits may attest to the same band or camp. It is from the huti camps of the colonial Seminoles that the more familiar matrilocal clan camps of the ethnographic present (MacCauley 1887; Spoehr 1941) were to develop.

Seminole Domestic Economy

Archaeology at A-296 provides us with only a partial picture of Seminole domestic economy of the colonial period, and again we must refer to the narratives of Rolle and Bartram. Their observations suggest that the conceptual axis of the ancestral Creek pattern—the separation of male and female activities and duties—was still very much an organizing principle of early

Seminole life. Men were often absent from their villages hunting, trading, or pursuing recreation (Bartram 1955:95, 214, 251;
Rolle 1977:48, 52, 53). Herding cattle and other activities that
could be accomplished from horseback were also rapidly coming
to figure in the reckoning of male prestige as horses became an
important indicator of wealth (and status) (and for this reason
no doubt saddles figured prominently and expensively on English gift lists; see Grant to Board of Trade, January 13, 1766, in
Grant 1772). Men of the Alachua band did, however, assist in
some agricultural duties, including clearing fields to be planted
and patrolling the cornfields at night to frighten away maraud-
ing animals (Bartram 1955:170).

Women were often observed tending fields, less often "mod-
estly showing their faces" from the dooryard (Bartram
1955:181), and perhaps were engaged in a number of duties not
often observed by the early chroniclers. I do not mean to imply
that Seminole women of the era were merely cultural bystanders
or lacked the desire to better their lives. As early as 1764 the
Englishman Rolle (1977:12) was visited by Seminole women in
canoes bearing him gifts, and probably women transported
canoe loads of oranges, watermelons, and other produce a decade later to Spalding's Lower Store (Bartram 1955:251). Furthermore, as Anglo traders became more numerous on the
Florida frontier, certain women were not long in exercising fem-
inine charms among them, especially if they themselves or their
families stood to gain. For their part, the traders often appear to
have wanted such unions because they would promote needed
alliances between themselves and the Indians. However, the
consequences of these alliances were not always positive, as
Bartram recounts in a woeful tale of a trader who got more, or
less, than he had bargained for:

> He is at this time unhappy in his connections with his beautiful
> savage. It is but a few years since he came here, I think from
> North Carolina, a stout genteel well-bred man, active, and of a
> heroic and amiable disposition; and by his industry, honesty, and
> engaging manners, had gained the affections of the Indians, and
> soon made a little fortune by traffic with the Seminoles; when un-

fortunately meeting with this little charmer, they were married in the Indian manner. He loves her sincerely, as she possesses every perfection in her person to render a man happy. Her features are beautiful, and manners engaging. Innocence, modesty, and love, appear to a stranger in every action and movement; and these powerful graces she has so artfully played upon her beguiled and vanquished lover, and unhappy slave, as to have already drained him of all his possessions, which she dishonestly distributes amongst her savage relations. He is now poor, emaciated, and half distracted, often threatening to shoot her, and afterwards put an end to his own life. [Bartram 1955:110]

Gender-prescribed roles continued to be important among the Seminoles, as they were among the Creeks, while the other important orientation for Seminole socioeconomic life was provided by the nuclear family.[4] As I have already suggested, Seminole hamlets of the period were in essence Creek huti, or neighboring households of clan-related women, and the huti formed an essential unit of land tenure and labor. However, trade activities, perhaps initially mediated in the squareground through the office of the chief, were apparently to be conducted eventually by nuclear families, who essentially acted as their own agents.

Bartram (1955:205) recalled meeting a Talahoschte man on the trail with his wife and children, leading a string of fine packhorses laden with barbecued meat, hides, and honey. On another occasion, he visited the "White Captain" and his family in their encampment near the store of a St. Johns River trader (Bartram 1955:110). Ten years earlier along the St. Johns, the Indian Philoki, with his wife and two sons, repeatedly visited the traders Rolle and Spalding, seeking their favor (Rolle 1977:30). Even the venerated Alachua chief Cowkeeper preferred to travel with his family and retinue to St. Augustine to meet privately with Governor Grant and shunned the formal Anglo-Indian congress at Picolata in October 1765.

The British, however, preferred not to treat with individual Indians, and in several instances Governor Grant became alarmed at the close relationship developing between Spalding and Philoki (Grant to Rolle, March 21, 1764, in Rolle 1977:20).

Grant correctly perceived the dangers that an uncontrolled frontier presented to his colony, one governed only by the desires of
entrepreneurs to line their pockets. Consequently his trading
policy included the stipulation that each Indian town would be
within the territory of only one licensed trader, to prevent competition and factionalism. Among the traders, however, competition was keen to secure rights to new and "uncaptured"
towns; among the Indians, incentive was provided to found
new towns via a fissioning process.

Seminole Beliefs and Ritual

The documentary record allows only a fleeting glimpse of
Seminole belief systems during the colonial period but enough
to temper the suggestion that Seminole religion was a simplified
form of Creek beliefs and rituals (Fairbanks 1978:174).

The black drink continued to have sacred importance, as did
tobacco smoking in the calumet, or ceremonial pipe of peace
(Bartram 1955:200). Busk ceremonies are not described in detail,[5]
but the practices of the residents of Cuscowilla with respect to
scrupulous village cleanliness and trash disposal suggest some
concern with the purity rites (Bartram 1955:169). The Seminole
concern for purity is also demonstrated by the observation that
they kindled new fires in the squareground to herald special
events (Bartram 1955:200), preserving the ancient southeastern
association between fire and renewal. The ball game mentioned
earlier between the Alachua and Suwannee Seminole (Rolle
1977:52) occurred during a twelve-day visit in May 1764, suggesting that additional ceremonies may have been involved.

An occurrence in the Indian town of Alachua (Latchaway) in
the same year indicates that the purity/pollution dichotomy held
far-reaching implications for everyday Seminole life. In a
drunken rage, Neatohowki, a nephew of Cowkeeper, grabbed a
glass bottle (allegedly obtained from Spalding) and quite literally
knocked out the brains of another Indian. Neatohowki dragged
his victim a short distance into the woods, where he remained
unburied because the Indians were "much afraid of the spirits of

these victims sacrificed to their passions" (Rolle 1977:48). The villagers would not handle the corpse and soon moved their houses some distance away from the spot where it lay.

The Seminole world was one inhabited by a panoply of powerful but invisible spirits. Men like the Long Warrior (Bartram 1955:215) commanded respect because of their ability to communicate with the spirits and summon them up on the individual's behalf. The white man's God was made more palatable to the Indian soul when he was described as the one "who thundered" (Rolle 1977:13). A precarious balance between good and evil existed in the Indian world. It was forbidden to harm creatures like the rattlesnake because such an action might incite the animal's fellows to seek revenge (Bartram 1955:220). In the "sympathetic" perspective of the Indians, an individual that interacted with powerful forces himself became more powerful, sometimes dangerously so. Thus when the naturalist William Bartram killed a large rattlesnake that had crawled into the Indian camp, they desired to bleed him to restore his former mild nature and became alarmed when he refused their treatment (Bartram 1955:218, 219).

The Seminoles invested their everyday behaviors with ritual or religious dimensions foreign to the European experience. What was secular business to the European colonists for the Indians at times held religious or sacred meaning. One such instance occurred at the Congress of Picolata, a meeting between the British and the Indians held on the banks of the St. Johns on November 15–18, 1765. Although this was the first and last time the Indians and colonists would meet under these circumstances (Miller and Hamell 1986), the events at Picolata clearly reveal native perceptions of the contact experience.

During the fall of 1765, Governor Grant summoned the "headmen and warriors of the Upper and Lower Creek towns to a congress in hopes of gaining from them boundary concessions with respect to lands east of the St. Johns.[6] Furthermore, Grant hoped to demonstrate the benevolence and goodwill of his new colonial administration by distributing presents should things go well and the Indians accept his terms (the goods were conveniently stored just offshore on the *East Florida* schooner until such an outcome was assured). On hand for the occasion were some fifty Indians (excepting Cowkeeper, who, as mentioned, waited until the following month to pay Grant a personal visit) and the naturalist John Bartram, accompanied by his son William, who was to return to Florida ten years later and write his famed narrative. The following account of the Picolata Congress is reconstructed from John Bartram's observations, entitled "Remarks on Ye Congress Held in a Pavilion" (J. Bartram 1942:51).

At the pavilion grounds the Indians assembled in two columns, facing at some distance Governor Grant and the Indian superintendent, John Stuart, seated inside the building. Six Indians in one of the columns carried in their arms gifts of twenty dressed buckskins. In the other column, a chief carried the calumet pipe hung with eagle feathers, and another carried a rattle box. These two individuals, probably Captain Aleck of a red Yuchi town and Tallachea of the white "Ockmulgies" (see Fairbanks 1974:149–152) were accompanied by an interpreter. Both columns advanced toward the pavilion in a timed, halting step, occasionally dancing, singing, and shouting. Within twenty paces of the pavilion, the procession halted for about five minutes, and suddenly the two chiefs carrying the pipe and rattle broke from the ranks and danced rapidly alone toward the English. The faces of Grant and Stuart were stroked with the eagle feathers from the calumet, and then the chiefs returned to the waiting columns of Indians. After speaking briefly with them, one chief returned to the pavilion, shook hands with the English, and presented them with the skins. The calumet pipe was lighted and smoked by Grant, Stuart, and the two chiefs, and the ceremony was concluded.

As a result of the proceedings, the Indians acquiesced to the boundary terms, and presents were distributed. The gifts included quantities of beads, ammunition, kettles, items of cheap hardware, and several saddles. Indian concerns for propriety were acknowledged, and their war and peace leaders had been received by men of equivalent rank among the English. Furthermore, the Indian portion of the ceremony had served native purposes well because it defined the English presence in their own terms. For example, the faces of Grant and Stuart were stroked with an eagle feather, a practice reminiscent of the Creek naming ceremony wherein a boy would don a feather on his head and would thus become like an adult warrior (Swanton 1928b:571). The combined presence of the symbolic calumet (Hall 1977:502) and eagle feathers (Hudson 1976:163) further reflected the Indians' desire for peace and for establishing a world in which some semblance of their own order prevailed. The Picolata account and other narratives of the period suggest that at this time the Indians were willing to accept the Europeans into their cosmos, whose order was based on dichotomies of purity, balance, and similarity. For a time, the white man found himself favorably ensconced in the native taxonomy.

Oven Hill, An Early Seminole Town

Referring again to the talwa system of the colonial Seminole, we should recall that the site of A-296 was interpreted as the remains of an outlying family homestead, whose nucleus was the town of Cuscowilla. Before Cuscowilla was founded in the early 1770s, the main Seminole towns in the area were Alachua, or Latchaway, the mother town of Cuscowilla on the border of the Alachua savanna, and the town of the White King on the west bank of the Suwannee. This latter town was visited in May 1764 by Denys Rolle (1977:50), accompanied by an Indian interpreter and a trader named Barnet who was then operating a store on the outskirts of Cowkeeper's Alachua settlement. The small party crossed the Suwannee in an Indian canoe and then traveled one-quarter of a mile overland to the town of the White King and his Savannah Indians.[7] Three years later the site was again visited by Lieutenant Pittman of the British service (Fairbanks 1974:161). Remains of this town were identified as an underwater component in the Suwannee by John Goggin in 1958 and were later described briefly as the Oven Hill site (8Di15) (Gluckman and Peebles 1974:25). Thus archaeology at the Oven Hill site complements our historical reconstruction of the Seminole talwa by providing a look at the material culture of an early Seminole town.

Collections from Oven Hill have long been famous among students of Florida archaeology because they contain the largest sample of Seminole pottery vessels known, most of which were recovered from the bottom of the Suwannee by Goggin and his student scuba divers. Vessel forms are diverse but typical of those found in late prehistoric domestic assemblages throughout the Southeast (see Hally 1986:282–284). Globular jars are the most common form and are either round or flat bottomed. Of twelve jars examined for various attributes (see table 3) the largest has an orifice diameter of 37 cm and was probably used for storage (see Hally 1986:285). The remaining eleven jars have orifice diameters ranging from 11 cm to 18 cm and were probably used to cook small portions of food. Nine of the twelve jars had brushed exteriors, and three are plain. Jars are the only vessel form at Oven Hill to have brushing. There does not appear to be a significant correlation between rim style, surface treatment, and orifice diameter in jars. Rim styles include notched ($n = 3$), notched fillet ($n = 2$), punctated ($n = 1$), and plain ($n = 6$) (figure 4). These rim styles can also be identified in the late prehistoric and historic Lamar series pottery associated with Creek peoples in Alabama (Dickens 1979; Knight 1985). Because the Oven Hill remains are attributable to a town center and not a family homestead, greater variability in rim styles is to be expected, as members of a number of different clans undoubtedly resided in or around the squareground.

Bowls are small (< 17 cm diameter), rounded or large (> 28 cm diameter), and carinated. Four of the sixteen vessels examined are bowls; two rounded (one a flat bottom, with a flaring rim form, and one with a round bottom) and two carinated. These four vessels have undecorated rims and smoothed surfaces. An additional large sherd from a carinated bowl bears incising clearly of the Lamar Incised type (Knight 1985:125, 158, 189; figure 5), again emphasizing the cultural connection between the Seminole and Creek traditions. The function of the rounded bowls can be inferred from Rolle's (1977:50) comment that he was served a bowl of china-briar root (*Smilax* spp.) soup during his visit to the "little Savannah" (Oven Hill) settlement. In addition he was served a dish of venison dressed with bear's

Table 3. Attributes of Selected Oven Hill pottery

FSM catalog no.	OD	H	T	RS	ST	VF	F
00027	13	14	s/ls	notched	brushed	jar	storage?
00002	18	21	s/ls	notched fillet	brushed	jar(r)	storage?
00006B	37	24	s/ls	notched fillet	brushed	jar	storage?
00019	12	17	s/ls	plain	smooth	jar	cooking?
2073	11	10	s/ls	plain	smooth	jar	?
00001	18	19	s/ls	notched	brushed	jar(f)	storage?
00020	12	8	s/ls	plain	smooth	jar(f)	?
Di15R	11	19	s/ls	plain	brushed	jar(f)	storage?
00010	14	14	s/ls	plain	brushed	jar(f)	storage?
00004	16	17	s/ls	plain	brushed	jar(r)	storage?
00012	18	19	s/ls	punctate	brushed	jar(r)	?
00009	16	12	s/ls	notched	brushed	jar(f)	?
00021	11	10	s/ls	plain	smooth	bowl(r)	cooking/serving?
00017	32	12	s/ls	plain	smooth	carinated bowl	?
00029	17	6	s/ls	plain	smooth	bowl(f)	cooking/serving?
00024	29	12	s/ls	plain	smooth	carinated bowl	cooking/serving?

Note: All measurements are in centimeters. OD = orifice diameter. H = height. T = temper. s/ls = sand and limestone tempering. RS = rim style. VF = vessel form. (f) = flat bottom. (r) = round bottom. ST = surface treatment. F = vessel function, as indicated by presence of interior pitting and/or exterior sooting (cooking?), and fire clouded exteriors with smoothed interiors and no pitting (cooking/serving?).

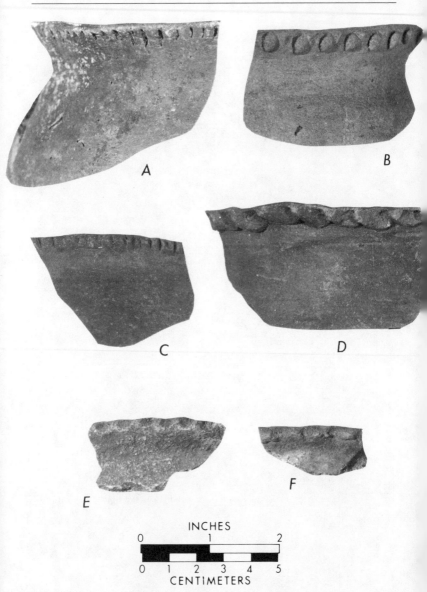

Figure 4. Selected Seminole rimsherds: A–D, Oven Hill; E, A-296; F, Spalding's Lower Store.

oil, which he perhaps consumed in a large carinated bowl. Such bowls were also used to heat foods over a fire, to judge from the fire-clouding present on vessel exteriors.

Bottles compose the third form class of the Oven Hill pottery. Orifice diameters of 8 cm and 10 cm were recorded for two bottles, both with complete orifices and portions of the shoulder intact. Rims are undecorated and vessel surfaces smooth. Oven Hill bottles, while few in number, are large in capacity and were probably used to store honey, bear's oil, and other commodities shipped by the Suwannee Seminoles to Cuba (Bartram 1955:194).

The classification of the Oven Hill pottery as to type raises taxonomic issues that have been little discussed with respect to Florida Seminole collections (Goggin 1958; Lewis 1969). A binomial, or type variety, system has recently been proposed for Creek ceramics in Alabama under the rubric of the Lamar series, in which attributes of paste and surface treatment serve to distinguish the different types and varieties (Knight 1985). Most of the incised, plain, brushed, and roughened (at least one sherd has a cob-marked exterior) sherds from Oven Hill can be comfortably grouped in the Lamar series and should be placed there, where they most closely express a real cultural relationship. A minority of sherds at Oven Hill suggest in their rim styles some affinity with the Florida mission period Leon-Jefferson series (H. Smith 1948; Willey 1949:490), an important indication that potters of this latter tradition may have been assimilated by the Seminoles. Further relations between mission and what were to become Seminole populations are indicated by a nearly complete vessel found near the Potano mission site at Fox Pond, Alachua County, bearing a Leon-Jefferson style notched rim and a brushed surface (the site of A-272, FSM Acc. A-1868, and see Mykel 1962). However, the combined qualities of vessel form, surface decoration, and stylistic treatment evidenced in the Oven Hill pottery suggest ceramic and culinary conservatism with respect to late prehistoric domestic pottery elsewhere in the Southeast. In its diversity and quantity the collection conforms to what we would expect of a village or town assemblage.

Figure 5. Seminole incised pottery: top, from Spalding's Lower Store; bottom, from Oven Hill.

European items are not common at the site but do suggest that the Seminoles of the 1760s possessed the means to become consumers on the Florida frontier. Domestic goods include sherds of Spanish olive jars and English ceramics, while the underwater recovery of a ceremonial "spontoon" tomahawk (Lien 1986; see also Bartram's depiction of Long Warrior) indicates that native symbols of office were known to the Europeans and had become an element in their trade. Further contact with the colonial authorities is indicated by the presence of British military buttons, razors, knives, and gun parts—all items that appear on the list of gifts prepared by Governor Grant for distribution at the Picolata Congress (see Covington 1961).

Articles of personal adornment—buckles, silver cones, earrings, glass beads—and items of horse tack (Gluckman and Peebles 1974:27) indicate a degree of wealth at the site possibly correlated with its increasing importance in colonial trade and politics. That White King and other residents of the town appreciated their position of potential power and prosperity on the frontier is illustrated in this curious anecdote recounted by Rolle (1977:50) at the time of Rolle's visit there in May 1764. The town did not have a resident trader, as did the Latchaway settlement, so White King appealed to Rolle not to continue his journey to St. Marks, perhaps to settle instead among them after obtaining his license. Barnet, the Dutch trader from Latchaway who accompanied Rolle during this leg of the trip, quickly abandoned his companion in their camp near the Indian village and went to town to strike his own deal with the Seminoles. His purpose must have been to attract the Suwannee band to his trading store at Latchaway, since he was prohibited by law from establishing himself in two towns. After hearing him out, several of the Indians visited Rolle's camp uninvited and proceeded to rifle through his bag of supplies. Thinking fast, Rolle drew a map in the sand depicting the St. Johns and the location of his prospective settlement and store and encouraged the Indians to bring their goods to him. Clearly this was the very sort of intrigue that Grant wished to avoid and in which the Seminoles delighted. However, with the increased ability of individual Seminoles to deal with the likes of Rolle and Barnet came the demise of Indian leaders such as White King and Cowkeeper. While the traditional office of town chief was slow to be extinguished, the Seminoles' growing interest in and opportunity to participate in commercial enterprise was greatly to erode the foundations upon which traditional chieftaincy was based.

Enterprise,
1767–1821

During the period of enterprise new social trends were emerging among the Seminoles as the nuclear family grew increasingly distinct from the broader community with respect to economic activities, the accumulation of wealth, and obligations of inheritance and descent. This process received some impetus from the British "one trader, one town" policy, which placed a premium on the founding of new towns by ambitious individuals and their families. Hereditary chiefs had little role to play in this new social order. Thus the Seminoles with which the Americans were to come in contact in the early 1800s were in reality (although not always in title) steered by a new breed of leader, individuals who possessed proven skill in negotiating in their own self-interest. Because by the second and third decades of the 1800s there was a plurality of Indian interests abounding in Florida, no single individual emerged who was qualified in the Indian minds to speak for all. Indeed, as I mentioned earlier, this was not the Seminole way.

The archaeological correlates of the period of enterprise are, first, the proliferation of sites that occurred as the Seminoles radiated across the Florida landscape in search of advantage and opportunity, and, second, the visibility of such sites, littered with an abundance of European porcelains, utilitarian earthenwares, colored glass beads, gunflints, pipestems, and a complete inventory of metal tools, utensils, and containers (figure

6). With the period of enterprise we have our first substantive look at the Seminole quotidian, while, unfortunately, our knowledge of the cosmological suffers somewhat.

The signal events opening the period of enterprise were the founding of the towns of Talahoschie, Cuscowilla, the Palatka town on the St. Johns River, and the settlements in the vicinity of Chukochatty (near present-day Brooksville, Hernando County), all during the years 1767–1772. By 1774 there were nine major Seminole towns dotted across the peninsula (Bartram 1955:367); by 1821 this number had increased fourfold (Fairbanks 1974:245).

Talahoschte has been mentioned previously in connection with Bartram's entertainment there by White King in 1774. At that time, the settlement was located on the east bank of the Suwannee (figure 1), north of Manatee Springs in the vicinity of Clay Landing (Levy County). Ten years earlier, White King was residing in the "Savannah" village on the west bank of the river, somewhat upstream from the 1774 location and in the vicinity of the Oven Hill archaeological site (8Di15). White King was visited here by Rolle and Barnet in 1764 and again by Lieutenant Pittman in 1767 (Fairbanks 1974:161). Between the years 1767 and 1774 the west bank site was abandoned by the White King in favor of the Talahoschte location, where he and his people constructed their village following the traditional Creek squareground plan.

Before he moved to Talahoschte the White King did not have a trader residing in his town, so that the Indians were prompted to incite an intrigue between Rolle and Barnet as previously noted. The White King was successful in attracting a resident trader to the Talahoschte town for a time, but this individual retreated to the relative safety of the St. Johns River when a traveler by the name of M'Gee was murdered by a band of Indians and tensions mounted in the colonial hinterlands. Bartram accompanied this man on his return to the village in 1774 to reestablish ties and to reclaim the string of packhorses that he had left behind in his flight (Bartram 1955:201). Upon his return, the trader found his former quarters occupied by a Seminole family. Through the means of a council and a treaty, the White King rec-

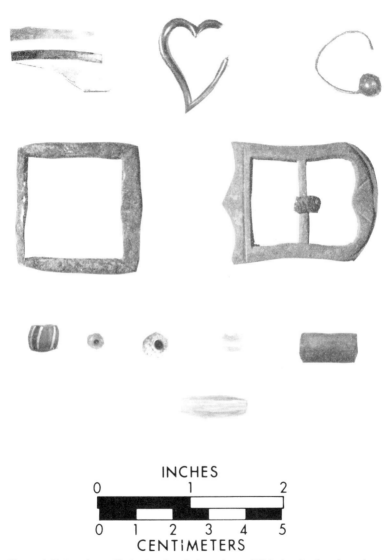

Figure 6. Enterprise artifacts: top, banded pearlware (Nicholson), silver brooch, earring (Spalding's); middle, metal belt buckles (Spalding's, A-296); bottom, glass beads (Nicholson).

onciled his people with the trader, assuring him that "every possible means should constantly be pursued to prevent any disturbance in [the] future on their part" (Bartram 1955:201). The White King's role as mediator of town affairs is clearly demonstrated, but again, it is important to realize that his authority, such as it was, extended little beyond the limits of the town square.

With an eye toward trade, we may conjecture as to the reason behind the move of White King's Seminoles from the west to the east bank of the Suwannee. Traders, and Indians wishing to trade, traveled overland at that time in packhorse trains. Licensed ferry operations made it possible to cross the broad St. Johns River in several places, but such transport was not available on lesser rivers such as the Suwannee. There travelers crossed by means of Indian canoes left on the banks for the purpose (both Rolle and Bartram were conveyed across the Suwannee in this fashion). For traders whose primary supply outlets were at the St. Johns River depots, it was inefficient, time consuming, and even perilous to transfer quantities of goods from pack train to canoe. The same situation pertained for Indians desiring to transport goods to the St. Johns River, as we know they did. Because the St. Johns stores (for example, Spalding's two ventures) were located on the west, or "Indian shore,"[1] trading could be conducted more easily between these points and locations in the interior, provided the latter were east of the Suwannee (see figure 1). With these conditions in mind, it is conceivable that the White King and his prospective trading partner hit upon a plan to resettle the Indians on the east bank, on the site that came to be known as Talahoschte. Inconveniences of the move would be minor compared with the potential benefits of freer, easier enterprise with the colonists, while the lucrative maritime commerce in which the Seminoles engaged with the Spaniards of Cuba (Bartram 1955:193, 194) would not be hindered.

At about the time of the founding of Talahoschte, the original Latchaway village was abandoned by Cowkeeper's Seminoles and the new village of Cuscowilla was constructed several miles to the south of the former town and near the present site of Micanopy. Upon his visit to Cuscowilla in 1774, Bartram (1955:169) learned, probably from Cowkeeper himself, that the "ancient" site had been abandoned because of the "stench of putrid fish" and the nuisance created by droves of biting mosquitoes. The location of Latchaway is uncertain, although several lines of evidence suggest that it may have been along the southwestern margin of the Alachua savanna, or what is now called Paynes Prairie. From Rolle's account of his visit to Latchaway (the only extant description of this village), we know that the trader Barnet had established himself in the vicinity by 1764; Barnet's post may have been the "former store" noted by Bartram and depicted by him on a map of the Alachua area (Bartram 1958:plate 21). In this same location is the archaeological site of A-362 (Mykel 1962), where Seminole pottery, sherds of English creamware, and kaolin pipe fragments were found in surface collections.

However, by 1774 trade with the Indian centers of Talahoschte and Cuscowilla had been interrupted because of certain "Indian troubles" in the north peninsula at that time. Grievances between the whites and the Seminoles had just been redressed at a treaty held in St. Augustine, and normal relations were to be reestablished with the traveling delegation that included Bartram, traders, and colonial representatives. Feasting, drinking the black drink, and smoking the pipe of peace took place in the town squares of both Cuscowilla and Talahoschte.

To understand why Cuscowilla was founded at about the same time as Talahoschte we must consider the locations of the interior Indian towns with respect to the trade routes inland from the St. Johns and fluctuations in the water level of the great Alachua savanna.[2] First, with the establishment of Talahoschte, the most direct route between it and the St. Johns River (in the vicinity of present-day Palatka) would be the most direct; this path would cross the margin of the Alachua prairie itself, provided the prairie was dry. In fact, by Bartram's time the road diverged just east of the prairie, with one fork leading around to the south and through Cuscowilla and the other crossing the southern margin of the prairie and possibly passing the original site of Latchaway. However, if changing water levels in the prairie made this latter passage difficult, or unpredictable,[3] the residents of Latchaway may have found themselves in danger of being bypassed by pack trains eager to make for the Suwannee and may have found their own travel becoming less and less convenient. Even within the last century, the prairie has filled to become a lake sufficient to float paddlewheelers and has drained again to its present condition. Thus in 1764 when Cowkeeper desired to parlay with Rolle and the trader Barnet not in the town of Latchaway but at a point one mile distant on the road to St. Marks (Rolle 1977:53), the move away from the Latchaway center may already have been under way. Whatever the specifics, the founding of the Seminole towns of Talahoschte and Cuscowilla around 1770 cannot be grasped apart from political and economic considerations as the Indians understood them.

A third Seminole town to be established during this time was located on the west bank of the St. Johns, near Palatka in what is now Putnam County. Bartram provides a picturesque description of the site, as viewed from the river:

> There were eight or ten habitations, in a row, or street, fronting the water, and about fifty yards distant from it. Some of the youth were naked, up to their hips in the water, fishing with rods and lines; whilst others, younger, were diverting themselves in shooting frogs with bows and arrows. On my near approach, the little children took to their heels, and ran to some women who were hoeing corn; but the stouter youth stood their ground, and, smiling, called to me. As I passed along, I observed some elderly people reclined on skins spread on the ground, under the cool shade of spreading oaks and palms, that were ranged in front of their houses. [Bartram 1955:95, 96]

Around the village were several hundred acres of cleared ground, including plantings of corn, potatoes, beans, squash, and melons and a carefully pruned orange grove. Melons and oranges were popular produce of the Indian trade and, as I noted earlier, became for women somewhat equivalent to furs and skins for men. Bartram was later to visit this town by land (Bartram 1955:250, 251), where he was entertained in a centrally located raised and canopied pavilion, decorated with dyed split-cane mats.

This village was located some twelve miles north of Spalding's Lower Store (the latter identified as the archaeological site of 8Pu23, near Astor) in the vicinity of Rollestown, where Denys Rolle was to establish himself tenuously during the years 1765–1770. To judge from Rolle's account (1977) and from records of the British Colonial Office, there was no major Seminole occupation in the area prior to Rolle's settlement; principal dealings were with the Alachua and Suwannee bands of Seminoles. However, Rolle's presence on the St. Johns provided the stimulus necessary for attracting Seminole settlers to the area; in particular one Philoki and his family, who evidently hoped to install themselves in the graces of both Rolle and Spalding. Their particular items of commerce were more the product of the field than of the forest, hence the extensive area of cultivated land surrounding the new town.

Thus by the year 1770, three new Seminole towns emerged in the north peninsula whose foundings quite literally reflect Indian moves in the direction of enterprise. Native society, as it had been experienced by the colonial Seminoles, was undergoing a profound reordering, however. By 1774 the Seminole towns in the north peninsula were maintaining little political or ritual contact. The British realized that important policies (for instance, the Treaty of St. Augustine) could be disseminated only by visits they paid to individual towns. There would be no more solemn expressions of pan-Indian religion and cosmology for European eyes such as that which had occurred at Picolata in 1765. It is likely as well that the ball game was no longer played between teams from opposing towns. Traditional clan and moiety affiliations now had less influence in determining social success and prestige than did individual initiative and shrewdness: witness Philoki's moves on the St. Johns with respect to the traders Rolle and Spalding. Furthermore, with the increased ability of the Seminoles to accumulate personal wealth, the traditional southeastern Indian descent system of matrilineal inheritance may have declined some in practice.[4] Thus by 1820 it was possible for Opauney, a Seminole residing east of Tampa

Bay in the vicinity of Winter Haven (Polk County), to leave his vast real estate holdings and accumulated possessions (including cash) to his son, while his houses, orchards, and fields were destroyed in keeping with Creek custom (Dexter in Glunt 1930:281).

The archaeological record indicates that the Seminoles still furnished their dead with grave goods, as did the Creeks and other southeastern Indians well back into prehistory. At the Zetrouer site (8A66) just east of the Alachua savanna (near the present site of Rochelle, Alachua County), excavators uncovered the remains of a Seminole male, flexed on his left side, head facing east, with an iron trade tomahawk and iron knife on top of his chest and a glass mirror tucked just under his knees (Goggin et al. 1949). In front of his legs were the remains of probably three pouches, two containing shot and flints and one containing powder. Around his waist had been a leather buckled belt (figure 6). Just above the heels was an inverted brass kettle; other possessions, including two more brass buckles, several coils of copper wire, red and yellow paint, an iron knife, a file and rasp, two pocket clasp knives, and a gun lock, had been placed at his back. Conspicuously absent, however, are glass beads, a common component of earlier and later domestic and mortuary assemblages, and the musket that the individual must have possessed.

This man was probably a resident of an outlying hamlet associated with Cuscowilla. The burial goods compare favorably with trade items excavated at the site of Spalding's Lower Store, operating in about 1763–1783 on the St. Johns (Lewis 1969). The individual buried at Zetrouer probably had commerce either directly with Spalding (remembering that Seminole sherds from the nearby 8A296 site excavated by Sears were stylistically similar to sherds recovered at Spalding's) or with the resident trader of Cuscowilla. Some idea of his relative wealth can be gained from table 4, based on information translated by Joseph Lockey from the Spanish AGI:PC Leg 2360.[5] A pound of skins equals eighteen ounces, and the measures of cloth are in Spanish yards. Figuring only those items that appear both on the trade list and with the burial, we can estimate that this individual was

Table 4. Trade items and their value in skins, 1783

Skins (lbs.)	Items
1	½ lb. powder, 40 bullets, 4 lbs. wool binding, 5 strings barley grain seeds, 5 strings common beads, 10 strings white enameled beads
1–3	knives, according to size
1–5	looking glasses, according to size
1–6	hatchets, according to size
2	silver earbobs
2–3	silver broach, 1 yd. white linen, handkerchiefs, 1 yd. baize cloth
3–4	1 yd. of finer linen
4	1 yd. stroud fabric
4–5	gingham shirt, 1 yd. chintz fabric, plain bridle
4–6	plain shirt
6	blanket with 1 stripe
6–7	double bridle
6–8	black silk handkerchief
8	stroud blanket
8–10	white ruffled shirt
16–18	ordinary trading gun
30–60	riding saddle

Note: Measures of cloth are in Spanish yards. One lb. = 18 ounces.
Source: Lockey n.d., AGI:PC Leg 2360.

buried with the trade equivalent of at least thirty-four pounds of skins, although this figure is undoubtedly conservative.

The skin trade was not the only enterprise open to the Seminole entrepreneur. After the demise of the British plantation system and their retrocession of Florida to Spain in 1783, there developed a real need for an interior breadbasket to provide food for the Spanish colonists. In line with this need, a new wave of Muskogee-speaking Upper Creek settlers moved just north and east of Tampa Bay (Swanton 1922:403). In this region of fertile, well-drained soils and ample savanna lands, a series of Seminole plantations developed at the hands of these Creeks, plantations that were to bring their owners no small measure of prosperity by the time Florida became an American territory in 1821.

The most informative account of these villages appears in a letter sent to Territorial Governor William P. Duval by Horatio S. Dexter in 1823. Dexter, by vocation a trader and merchant and one-time representative of the speculative Alachua Company, was also something of a frontier diplomat and was employed by Duval to inform the peninsular Indians of an upcoming council at Moultrie Creek.[6]

Dexter traveled from St. Augustine to Volusia, then on to the Indian settlement of Okahumpka, where Micanopy, nephew of the late King Payne of the Alachua Seminoles and now their leader, resided. Twelve miles south of Okahumpka was Pilaklikaha, where Micanopy's one hundred black slaves were settled. This location is between the present towns of Bevilles Corner and Center Hill, Sumter County. Here one hundred acres were under cultivation in corn, rice, and the "ground nut," or peanut. Leaving Pilaklikaha, Dexter traveled twenty-eight miles southwest to the settlement of Chukochatty (variously spelled), also known as Red House, Red Town, or New Eufala (near the present city of Brooksville, Hernando County), settled by migrants from the Creek town of Eufala in eastern Alabama as early as 1767 (Swanton 1922:403). At the time of Dexter's visit, Simaka was the town chief and owned 3 slaves, 160 head of cattle, 90 horses, and a number of hogs. The prosperity of this settlement was so marked that two years prior to Dexter's visit 60 black slaves residing there were lost in a Creek raid from the north.

Twelve miles south of Chukochatty, Dexter entered a village on the border of a lake where corn, pumpkins, and watermelons were grown. Four miles farther was the settlement of Toma-hitche, a series of dispersed hamlets situated so as to take advantage of the savanna pasturage in the area. The hamlets shared a common field planted in corn and rice. These settlements were just southwest of present-day Dade City (Pasco County), on the highlands west of Lake Pasadena. From here Dexter continued south, crossing the Hillsborough River and entering the village of Hechapauka, or Hich-a-pue-sesse (Fairbanks 1974:246), where peach and "Pride of India " trees were said to have flourished. Its inhabitants had previously dispersed to the villages of Chukochatty, Tomahitche, and Tophokilika (the latter presumably near the central Florida lake of the same name).

Traveling south and southeast, Dexter then crossed Alafia Creek (noting that the peninsula south of this point was regarded as Indian hunting territory) and reached Opauney's plantation (figure 1) on the west side of Lake Hancock. Here Opauney lived much in the manner of a proper Anglo-American planter. His two-story frame house was surrounded by a corn house, dairy, stable, and other outbuildings. Also on the site was a "physic" house, containing sacred war medicines for use only by a medicine man. The presence of this building suggests that despite its outward resemblance to, perhaps, an English or American plantation, Opauney's settlement retained vestiges of its native roots. His extensive plantings were of corn, potatoes, an orchard of peaches, and rice. Opauney maintained a thriving rice export business with Spanish St. Augustine and had managed to accumulate seven thousand dollars in cash by the time of his death in 1823. After touring the vicinity of Opauney's town, Dexter returned to St. Augustine via Pilaklikaha, Okahumpka, and Volusia.

The Nicholson Grove Site (8Pa114)

The archaeology of Seminole sites of this period indicates that domestic consumption was nothing short of ostentatious. At the Nicholson Grove and Hawes sites (probably Dexter's Tomahitche) west of Lake Pasadena in Pasco County (figure 1), the plentiful surface collections of trade artifacts suggest that here Seminole enterprise was at its zenith. Both sites, on adjacent knolls in long-cultivated orange groves, are defined by a surface scatter of artifacts some 150 m in diameter. Systematic collecting has been conducted on the sites over the past several years by amateur archaeologists from Dade City.

The most striking aspect of the Nicholson collection is the

quantity of European glass trade beads present (figure 7). In quantity (there are at least fifty) and variety the Nicholson bead sample dramatically contrasts with domestic assemblages from earlier and later periods of Seminole history and is only equaled by collections made from Seminole living sites of this century in south Florida (see, for example, the type collection assembled by John Goggin and now housed at the Florida State Museum). Easily identifiable beads include the familiar red over green "Cornaline d'Aleppo" (type IV A2 in the Brain 1979 taxonomy, and occur throughout the Southeast on sites dating between 1600 and 1836, with a mean date of 1727 (Brain 1979). Varieties of monochromatic faceted beads that become popular after the turn of the nineteenth century (Smith 1979:170 in Dickens 1979) are also found at Nicholson. Another Nicholson specimen that appears in the bead literature is a round, drawn polychrome bead (see figure 6) described from French-influenced sites in the Southeast (Gregory and Webb 1965:33–39; Brain 1979:107, his type IV B7). These three types of beads evidently remained popular among the Seminoles through the 1830s and appear both as items of personal adornment included with Seminole burials dating to the 1830s at the military post of Fort Brooke (Piper and Piper 1982) and, probably, as components of the colorful, multibead necklaces drawn by the artist Catlin in his portraits of the Seminoles (see Fundaburke 1958).

Quantities of European tablewares are also present, including shell-edged (at Hawes) and transfer-print (Nicholson) pearlwares and banded wares (figure 6). European red and green glazed earthenwares are also included in the collections. At least one ceramic teapot was in use at Nicholson, and one complete tea setting may be represented by the collected sherds (figure 8).

Native pottery is represented by Chattahoochee Brushed sherds, and specimens of a plain, sand-tempered ware. One shoulder sherd from a cazuela bowl bears gashlike punctations identical to treatments appearing in contemporaneous historic Creek collections (Dickens 1979:122, 131). Thus far, punctated, incised, or notched fillet styles of rim treatment are not known from Nicholson; however, the strong and direct continuity between Creek and Seminole pottery traditions is clearly ex-

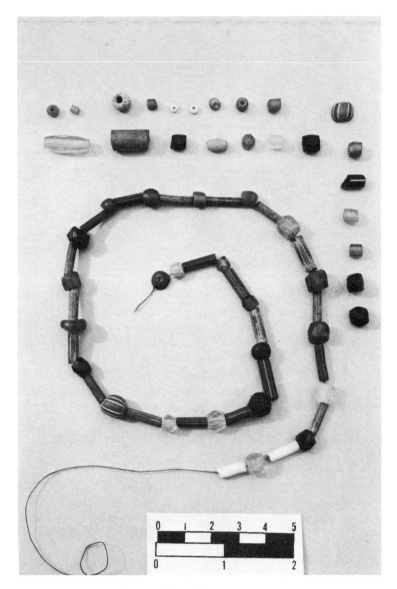

Figure 7. Glass beads from Nicholson Grove

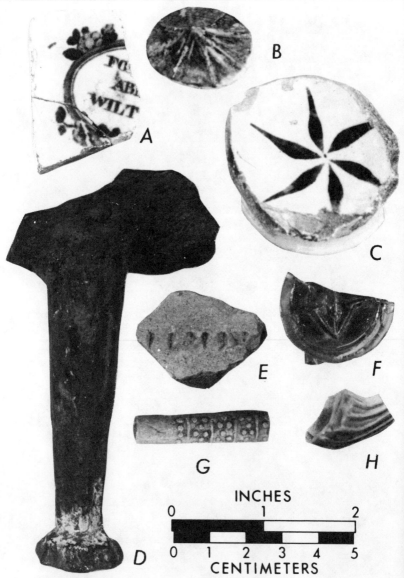

Figure 8. Nicholson Grove artifacts: A–C, European ceramics; D, "Dutch Oven" leg; E, pottery; F, bottle seal; G–H, clay pipe fragments

pressed. Fragments of kaolin smoking pipes are abundant, including one stem portion (figure 8) of probable Dutch origin commonly found on French and Spanish colonial sites with an early nineteenth-century date. The leg from the presumed "Dutch Oven" resembles finds from a number of sites in the Creek area, while a different style of iron kettle was evidently imported into Florida through Spalding's store on the St. Johns (Lewis 1969:82).

Numerous bottle sherds occur at the sites, including a green glass bottle seal with an anchor motif (figure 8). Bottle glass sherds chipped for use as tools are also in the collections and would have been useful in skinning large animals such as cattle and deer. Hunting activities are further indicated by a number of gunflints in the Nicholson collections.

The combined assemblage from Hawes and Nicholson Grove (although the specific relationship between the two sites is not clear) illustrates two important points about the Seminole of the period of enterprise. First, the Florida peninsula was still perceived as a land of opportunity as late as the third quarter of the eighteenth century; families and in some cases towns of Creek immigrants, bearing with them a Creek material culture, positioned themselves in their new homes with respect to their commercial interests. Second, prosperity was forthcoming for these peoples, as their produce and products were packed off to Spanish St. Augustine (Griffin 1957), to the St. Johns trading houses, and to the Spanish store at Apalachee (Fairbanks 1974:126) or were bartered to subsidiary traders or peddlers mentioned in the Spanish documents of the time (Zespedes to Galvez, August 16, 1784, in Lockey 1945:254). Spanish goods were still at times sought out in Havana by Indian and trader alike because of their relative inexpensiveness. If we compare the Nicholson and Hawes sites to the Dexter manuscript, it is evident that the Seminoles here had an economy based on plantation crops grown in part for export (for instance, peaches and rice), complemented by animal husbandry for the same purpose. In exchange for Seminole goods, items were obtained in the hopes of demonstrating personal wealth and success (beads and pipes) and even a degree of household luxury (tea servings). The actual prepa-

ration and consumption of foods within the household probably
remained conservative in nature, thus the continued presence of
traditional Creek pottery on Florida Seminole sites.

Further Radiations of the Seminoles

Other Seminole sites of the period demonstrate the extent of
Seminole participation in the atmosphere of commerce provided
by the British and Spanish colonial governments. The Mizell site
(8Or14),located in an orange grove overlooking Lake Mizell in
Winter Park, contains numerous sherds of transfer-print and
blue shell-edged pearlwares, plain whitewares, banded wares,
brown glazed earthenwares, and kaolin pipe fragments. The
Seminole pottery type Winter Park Brushed was named and described on the basis of collections of aboriginal pottery from this
site (Goggin 1958); the distinction between it and Chattahoochee
Brushed rests on the small quantities of limestone included in
the Winter Park paste. Presumably the latter type is a Florida
variant of the Creek brushed pottery tradition; however, the
brushed Winter Park sherds included in the Mizell collection at
the Florida State Museum (Accession A-3036) closely resemble
samples of Chattahoochee Brushed. This resemblance suggests
that the type Winter Park Brushed needs some reevaluation and
perhaps can be simply included with Chattahoochee Brushed.
Although documentary references to the Winter Park Seminoles
are lacking, the Mizell site demonstrates the use of the central
Florida lake district by these Indians again in a situation favorable to plantation agriculture and animal husbandry.

Agriculture and animal husbandry were key economic practices of the Seminoles, but along the Florida Gulf coast other
bands were developing different strategies for gaining access to
the avenues of enterprise. As early as 1774 one group settled at
"Caloosahatchie" on the "bay of Calos" (Bartram 1955:194, 367)
(near present-day Fort Myers and Pine Island Sound, Lee
County) for the purpose of trading skins and furs to Spanish
fishermen who cured and salted their catch on the beach before
returning to Cuba. During the years 1774–1823 the coastal is-

lands from the area of Tampa Bay south to the vicinity of Charlotte Harbor became refuges for bands of Indians, "Spanish
Indians" (Sturtevant 1953; Neill 1955:43), and the so-called Seminole Negroes, all jockeying for position with respect to Spanish
trading and fishing vessels working the lower coast (Hammond
1973). The activities of these traders were not for the most part
sanctioned by the British Colonial Board of Trade during the
British period and after 1784 served to undermine the efforts of
the Spanish-sanctioned Panton, Leslie, and Company to bring
the coastal Indians within the sphere of Euro-Indian relations.
From this spirit of separatism, in terms of attitudes with regard
to both the interior Seminoles and the seat of colonial authority
in St. Augustine, were to develop individuals the likes of the
legendary Mikasuki Sam Jones, or Arpeika, whose small band of
intransigents survived two wars waged against them by the
United States to become one of the founding populations of today's Seminoles.

By 1822, a curious state of affairs existed on the central and
southwestern Gulf coast. Spanish maritime trade with the lower
peninsula was by now an established and lucrative enterprise
and had led to the development of bands of middlemen—well-
armed and near-piratical blacks—who lived on the outer islands
and interrupted free trade between the ships and the interior Indians. From the inland Seminoles—probably Opauney and others—they acquired cattle, which they exchanged for Spanish
goods obtained at the boats. Such activities alarmed Dexter,
who described the danger to Governor Duval with great concern. Dexter did not report, probably because he wanted to save
face as a self-styled Indian expert and diplomat, that by this time
the coastal bands included not only blacks but also Seminoles,
Spaniards, and the so-called Spanish Indians of mixed parentage. This second front of opportunity provided by the Indian
presence along the coast was not lost on several independent
English entrepreneurs, who opened stores in the vicinity of
Tampa Bay and points north. The most important of these operations, conducted by Alexander Arbuthnot and Robert Armbrister, sought to recruit Indians to their allegiance and thereby
to undermine the established channels of the Florida Indian

trade, now in the hands of John Forbes and Company. By 1818 Arbuthnot and Armbrister had introduced an uncertainty into white-Indian relations that threatened to disturb the peace, and they were captured and summarily executed in Spanish Florida by General Andrew Jackson of the U.S. Army (Fairbanks 1974:221–232).[7]

One archaeological site attributable to the coastal Seminoles is found on the Weeki Wachee River, north of Tampa Bay (figure 1). Here, in the upper component of a shell midden also containing remains from earlier Safety Harbor, Weeden Island, and Deptford archaeological cultures, there were recovered Spanish olive jar sherds; sherds of Staffordshire china and feather-edged pearlware; smoking pipe fragments; faceted blue glass necklace beads; red and blue "seed," or embroidery, beads; and bottle glass sherds (Ferguson 1976). The olive jar sherds suggest seaborne trade with Cuba, as they do not occur in any number on inland Seminole sites. The European pearlwares and the blue-faceted beads combine to suggest at least an early nineteenth-century occupation at the site by the Seminoles. Seminole pottery again indicates a Creek heritage, with the recovery of a brushed jar and a cazuela bowl with "ticked" decorations at its shoulder (see the similar treatment at Oven Hill, illustrated in figure 5; for a Lamar example in the Creek area, see Dickens 1979:179).

The trade items found at the Weeki Wachee site indicate that bands of coastal Seminoles were able to parlay either goods or services into desired goods and that this was perhaps most easily accomplished through a maritime exchange with Cuba. The American policy of containment recognized that control over the Florida Indians could be effected only when and if unrestrained use of the Gulf waters could be prevented; thus the Indian reservation created by the Treaty of Moultrie Creek (1823) had its bounds not closer than twenty-five miles to any coast (see Mahon 1967:endpiece). The exact fates of many of the coastal-oriented Seminole once Americans had come to control in Florida are not known. Arpeika and his band eluded capture through two wars and settled deep within the Everglades. The painting of his camp there done by Seth Eastman (see Swanton 1946:plate

79), dating to the late 1830s, indicates that an early form of "chickee" housing had been developed. The prototype of this familiar Seminole house form may have been constructed in Arpeika's coastal settlement north of Tampa Bay before the outbreak of the Second Seminole War. Other preadaptations to the southern Florida wetlands on the part of the peninsula Seminole may have been forged in the small coastal settlements as well.

The Demise of the Alachua Seminoles

Upon the death of Cowkeeper in the 1790s, the control of the Alachua band passed to his son, known to history as King Payne. Payne evidently abandoned the site of Cuscowilla and founded Paynestown (8Al366), approximately two miles to the northeast of the former location and within the bounds of what is now Paynes Prairie State Preserve.

Archaeological survey (Mykel 1962) and excavations (Mullins 1978:78–80) at the site of Paynestown suggest that this was not the formal squareground center that Cuscowilla had been but was constructed plantation style like Opauney's settlement east of Tampa Bay. The site of Payne's house was defined by a concentration of English ceramics, smoking pipe fragments, glass sherds, glass necklace beads, gun furniture, and Chattahoochee Brushed pottery. English ceramics include banded and transfer-print pearlwares, salt-glazed stoneware, and lead-glazed earthenware and together indicate that the site was occupied in about 1790–1820 (Mullins 1978:78). The absence of the large blue-faceted beads that became so popular with the Seminoles early in the nineteenth century suggests that the terminal occupation of Paynestown occurred well before 1820 and probably coincides with Payne's death at the hands of an invading Georgia militia in 1812.

Payne's house was surrounded by various outbuildings (or refuse pits), evidenced by smaller concentrations of European goods (including additional glass beads and a silver earring) and Chattahoochee Brushed pottery (these sherds are identified as Winter Park Brushed and Plain in the site report). Payne was clearly a man of some wealth. However, to judge from the archaeological survey results, he did not place himself or his residence at the center of a town like Cuscowilla (see Bartram 1955:168). Presumably other members of the Alachua band were scattered in hamlets throughout the southern hammocks of the prairie and thus by perhaps 1812 there is evidence for the diffuse or dispersed pattern of settlement that is so often discussed with regard to the Seminoles (Fairbanks 1978:175; Milanich and Fairbanks 1980:254; Dickinson and Wayne 1985:5–11). By the close of the period of enterprise, new circumstances were acting to exacerbate the noted trends of social fission and reorganization among the Seminoles. With the incursions of the Georgians and the death of Payne following a pitched battle near the eastern shore of Newnan's Lake, the nucleus of the Alachua Seminole band shattered. Cowkeeper's descendants dispersed to the corners of the peninsula, from the flight of the family of Bowlegs (Payne's brother) west of the Suwannee to the far reaches of southern Florida where Payne's family was to settle. A large group of blacks once associated with Sitarkey of the Alachua band moved south and west to the remote banks of the Withlacoochee, where Dexter was to supply them with sugarcane plants in 1822.

The prosperity of the Seminoles ultimately led to their demise. By their efforts industrious Seminoles demonstrated that the Florida sands could indeed be husbanded at a profit. In areas once considered too remote or infertile by the early European colonists, the Seminoles were successful in developing an export economy based on agropastoralism. They provided an example that was to appeal to the new breed of American pioneer, who hoped to make a decent living from the land with little or no capital outlay. It was difficult for these men to consider a life of economic competition with the Indians, although the Indians did not object at first to the settlers' presence as long as the Indians could engage with them in trade.

The conspicuous Seminole prosperity in Florida created a tempting target for raids by both whites and Indians (for instance, the Coweta Creek raid on the Seminole town of Chukochatty in 1819, in which numerous cattle, horses, and blacks were carried off); actions that provoked a cycle of troubled, unstable border conditions when the Seminoles sought, on occasion, to retaliate. This atmosphere was not conducive to American plans for the Florida territory, and so designs for a formal Indian policy included provisions for containment and removal.

It is also important to remember that the Florida Seminole population had increased about tenfold since Bartram's day, thereby suggesting to Americans the possibility that they would have to coexist with a strong, sovereign Indian nation operating according to its own wishes on American soil. This the Americans were not prepared to do. But Florida continued to act as a magnet of perceived opportunity for the southeastern Indians, and significant migrations occurred as late as 1814 (Sturtevant 1971:106).

Comparison of contemporaneous burials of Creeks (at Childersburg—see DeJarnette and Hansen 1960; for the Chattahoochee drainage, see DeJarnette 1975) and Seminoles (Zetrouer, 8A66, see Goggin et al. 1949) from the third quarter of the eighteenth century suggests that Indian perceptions had some foundation in fact: the personal wealth that could be accumulated by the Seminoles perhaps exceeded that to which their northern neighbors had access. The implications of this trend were evident to the Americans. Consequently the end of the period of Seminole enterprise was to coincide closely with the coming of American control to the Florida peninsula. Seminole enterprise did not entirely cease, for commercial activities with Spanish Cuba were to continue through the years of the Second Seminole War and beyond. Government-sanctioned Indian stores were maintained at military posts after the creation of the Indian reservation in 1823; here limited trading and even cash sales were permitted. But the Americans were, literally, not as hungry for Indian goods as the Europeans had been, and they saw less need to keep the peace.

Seminole Society at the Period's Close

During the years 1767–1821, the Seminoles significantly transformed the ancestral Creek pattern. Leadership became very local in scope and increasingly reflected ability, not inheritance. As traders and trade opportunities proliferated through the Florida peninsula, so did Seminole towns, founded by individuals and their families, who departed from the traditional talwa pattern of settlement organization. The real authority of the chief was undermined as people found that they could strike deals on their own.

Women's roles were enhanced as women found that they too could produce items of commercial value, especially crops such as watermelons, corn, rice, peaches, and oranges. Their bonds with other women of their clan were perhaps reinforced by such activities, and in some cases the huti were undoubtedly functioning as socially independent, economically autonomous units. Seminole women themselves achieved status in the eyes of both Indians and whites because through them important trade alliances could be established.

The traditional practice of matrilineal inheritance was undergoing revision, especially when large amounts of wealth were at stake. Upon the death of Opauney, his son appropriated three hundred head of cattle, one hundred packhorses laden with rice and other articles, and seven thousand dollars in currency, despite Dexter's assertion that Opauney's nephew should properly, according to custom, inherit.

Some syncretism had occurred between Christianity and native religion, perhaps because the Seminoles had on occasion assimilated Indian survivors from the earlier Spanish missions in their midst. The crucifix-wearing, Spanish-speaking Indians resident among the Cuscowilla Seminoles (Bartram 1955:164) were presumably descended from mission Indians. By the early 1800s the Seminoles believed in a Supreme Being, a positive entity, who existed in opposition to an evil spirit, who beckoned men to do wrong. Wrongdoers were banished after death to a nether world of eternal fire (Dexter in Boyd 1958). Such beliefs overlaid traditional beliefs and practices, where annual busk ceremonialism and the powers of the medicines prevailed. The Seminole cosmos was sufficiently plural in nature to accommodate a diversity of at times contrasting beliefs, and it remains so to this day.

The combined experience of the Florida Indians during this

period of enterprise marked the cultural passage from Creek to Seminole. The social and economic contexts of this era placed a premium on individual performance and achievement, attributes that are exhibited in the Seminole personality of the ethnographic present. They were now to face the American presence in their Florida homeland, an experience that would serve to reinforce the value of their received wisdom and traditional lifeways.

Revitalization, 1821–1841

The net cultural effect of the period of enterprise on Seminole society was the development of autonomous bands of self-willed indviduals. The implications were downscaling of traditional authority structures and a lack of singularity in leadership (Fairbanks 1974:265). No individual with the aplomb and savvy of the Creeks' Alexander McGillivray (Green 1980:41) would arise among the Seminoles, nor would the Seminoles have been likely to entrust such power to one man. Indeed, even McGillivray, whose unique brand of eighteenth-century shuttle diplomacy ensured for the Creeks at least temporary security on the southeastern frontier, failed to extend his authority over the Seminole bands in Florida when he was at the height of his power in 1790.

On the domestic scene, the Americans were attempting, with mixed results, to assess the numbers of Florida Indians and their locations and at times elicited testimony from native informants for this purpose (Fairbanks 1974:233–254). What the Americans called Seminole towns in reality contained as few as 12 and as many as 250 persons (Dexter in Boyd 1958; Fairbanks 1974:236). Furthermore, it is not clear whether in fact the noted population centers were true cultural entities or were instead artifacts of the census-taking procedure. Particularly south of the Suwannee, or within the bounds of our study area, the documents do not make clear the nature of the settlement patterns practiced by the

Seminoles. Because settlement patterns have much to do with social organization, it is difficult to estimate from historical sources just how the Seminoles structured their lives.

The first portion of this chapter will be concerned with chronicling the development of the so-called clan camp (Spoehr 1941:10, 14), which became for Seminoles of recent times the primary ordering principle of their daily lives. The evolution of the clan camp, and the development of a nativistic movement among the Seminoles during the years of the Second Seminole War, together emphasize one of the major trends in Seminole culture history—the Indians' ability to transform the antecedent cultural configurations of their own past into new and vital forms.

Ethnoarchaeology of the Seminole Clan

The prototype of the Seminole clan camp is the Creek huti (Swanton 1928b:171), or the local arrangement of matrilineally related households. Because residence after marriage was primarily matrilocal among the Creeks, new household compounds for the married couple were established in the vicinity of the wife's former residence. Her new family would enter into reciprocal and obligatory arrangements with her mother, her mother's sisters, and her own married sisters. These women were all of the same clan, as were all other members of the compounds except the husbands. Combined archaeological and ethnohistorical research in the Creek area suggests the presence of this settlement pattern by the mid-eighteenth century (Knight 1985:120), although it may have developed from the Mississippian hamlets of late prehistoric times.

The social history of the Seminoles is in a sense the story of how the clan camp evolved from antecedent forms of social organization. To understand this development, we must consider the centripetal and centrifugal forces influencing Seminole society through the course of its evolution. The early Seminoles who came into Florida were essentially Creeks—in their lifeways, cosmology, and social organization. The primary settlement pattern was a squareground center surrounded by affiliated hamlets. The hamlets probably contained people related through matrilineage and clan membership, as was the case in the Creek area. The hamlets became increasingly independent of the squareground centers because the traders tended to treat all Indians equally and thus diminished the power and authority of the town chiefs. Furthermore, the hamlets may have split along the lines of the nuclear family as increased opportunities for trade and prosperity presented themselves. Clan membership was perhaps at its lowest ebb during this period, and in fact there was little emphasis on social unity. This was the situation from about 1780 through the early 1820s.

The American presence in Florida was to alter this atmosphere of good feeling, and the centrifugal forces in Seminole society were reversed. Families began to draw together like "beads on a string" (Spoehr 1941:16); the string being the traditional clan affiliation. Incentives for trade under British and Spanish rule vanished with the American policy of containment (although Horatio Dexter and the Alachua Company attempted for a time to keep channels open by distributing gifts to Micanopy and other prominent indivduals; see Glunt 1930). The Treaty of Moultrie Creek, drawn up between the Seminoles and the Americans in 1823, required the Seminoles to move within the bounds of a central Florida reservation and there, after a time, to become self-sufficient. The prospect of such a lifestyle perhaps reinforced among the Seminoles the need to be allied with a group larger than the nuclear family and led to the reactivation of kinship bonds. In addition, the continued raiding of Seminole settlements by the Creeks, acting on their own or as mercenaries for other interests, may have suggested to the Seminoles that strength did indeed lie in numbers and that some degree of nucleation was advantageous. The new Seminole towns founded within the Moultrie Creek reservation after 1823 were in reality aggregates of small groups of individuals, bonded through matrilineage. The former situation in which neighboring households contained related women gave way to a residence pattern in which related women lived in the same household. This latter pattern is commonly known as the clan camp, of which Mac-

Cauley's (1887:507) is perhaps the first explicit description (see chapter 1). Fortunately, data derived from the archaeological ex cavations of Seminole burials at Fort Brooke and from domestic sites near the Withlacoochee River illuminate the processes of clan solidarity and the formation of the clan camp.

Clan Solidarity: The Fort Brooke Cemetery

With the outbreak of the Second Seminole War in 1835, the American attitude toward the Florida Indians rapidly became single-minded. All Indians not killed in the hostilities were to be caught and deported to Indian Territory west of the Mississippi River. Some individuals and their bands decided not to resist American directives and cashed in their Florida possessions in preparation for emigration. In one legendary case, after selling his cattle at the post at Fort King, Charley Emathla was met on the road and killed by Osceola, who discarded the coins in disgust (Charley Emathla suffered a fate similar to that of the Indian murdered in Latchaway in 1764; his body was left unburied on the road).

Fort Brooke, erected in 1824 to monitor activities on the newly created Indian reservation, became a major depot from which emigrating, or captured, Indians were boated west. The site of the cemetery located near the fort was excavated by the firm of Piper Archaeological Research, Inc., under contract with the City of Tampa prior to the city's construction of a municipal parking garage at the location. The burials excavated by the Pipers included the remains of thirteen adult Seminole males, eight adult Seminole females, and seventeen subadults. Several of the subadults had with them relatively large quantities of grave goods and items of personal adornment, suggesting to the excavators that clans were seeking to reinforce alliances between themselves by distributing gifts to deceased youths (Piper and Piper 1982:325; Piper, Hardin, and Piper 1982). In their view, this behavior was a cultural response to stress. While the clan is probably the appropriate unit of analysis, the evidence of Seminole ethnohistory suggests that the Seminoles had for some time placed a high value upon their youths. Therefore, the burial riches at Fort Brooke may reflect a practice of greater antiquity than the Second Seminole War. For example, as early as 1764 the Seminole Philoki was noted traveling to a St. Johns plantation with his "two sons well dressed" (Rolle 1977:30), while depictions of the young Osceola Nikkanoochee by Catlin in 1837 (Fundaburke 1958) show a young man dressed with crescentic silver gorgets, strands of glass beads, and the like (see Welch 1977 for an interesting, if slightly fabulous, biography of Osceola's alleged nephew).

However, organization of the Seminole burials at Fort Brooke into burial groups or lots (figure 9) suggests that the burial groups are of individuals related by clan. Grave lots were segregated on the basis of two parameters. Consistent alignment of graves was interpreted to mean that certain graves were intentionally placed next to each other, and sets or clusters of graves that met the above criterion were grouped separately if they were composed exclusively of Amerindian (to use the excavators' term) or Seminole remains (for related discussion of ethnic determination at the site, see Weisman 1985a). The burial groups are assumed to represent groups of individuals associated in life.

Two further assumptions must be presented before we proceed. First, because the burials at Fort Brooke were presumably done under military supervision, it must be assumed that the military respected the Indians' wishes to be buried in their clan lots. In fact, eyewitness accounts of several Indian burials in the cemetery (Prince 1836:October 13, in Prince 1836–1842; Piper and Piper 1982:30) suggest that the army was in general accepting of the Indians' requests. Second, we must assume that the burials were not simply arranged in rows consecutively upon death, so that no discretion could be exercised regarding the placement of individuals. However, terminus post quem dating based on coins found with persons buried at some distance from one another (burials 27 and 30) suggests that both interments may have occurred within the same period of time. This finding strengthens the assumption that all portions of the cemetery were in use at any given time.

FORT BROOKE CEMETERY
QUAD BLOCK SITE (8 Hi 998)

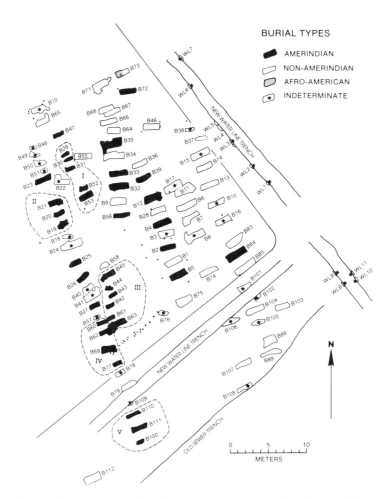

Figure 9. Burial groups at Fort Brooke cemetery. *Source:* After Piper and Piper 1982.

If the burial patterns at the Fort Brooke cemetery do in fact reflect a degree of native influence, rather than factors of conven-
ience or military practice, then they provide a useful cultural
datum from which to evaluate the evolution of Seminole behaviors with regard to the dead. In 1764, according to the Rolle
(1977) document, the Seminoles shared the southeastern Indian
aversion to the dead. The Latchaway village, or some portion of
it, was moved to place it at a greater distance from a corpse. Burials at this time were probably attended to by male relatives of
the deceased (Swanton 1928b:391, 393). Since many of the
Latchaway males were away in southern Florida on a hunting
trip, there was probably no one present in the village who could
properly handle the corpse. One burial practice common
throughout the Southeast in the eighteenth century was to en-
tomb the individual below the floor of his house (Swanton
1928b:391–395). With him were included personal possessions
that might be useful in the afterlife. In typical circumstances,
this procedure must have prevailed among the Alachua Seminoles, hence the observed features of the Zetrouer burial (Goggin et al. 1949) that I described earlier.

However, a different burial treatment existed among the historic Choctaws (then residing in what is now south-central Mississippi). The Choctaw dead were at first placed alone upon a
scaffold in the woods. After some time the bones were collected
and cleaned by the infamous "bone pickers." The cleaned bones
were then set in a box, which was placed with other boxes in a
mausoleum located in the town (Bartram 1955:403, 404). Sixteenth-century Spanish explorers recorded a similar custom in
native Florida and throughout the lower Southeast.

By 1818, scaffold burial was recorded among the Seminoles,
and another practice shared with the Choctaws—the construction of a log pen or stockade around the deceased (Young 1934–
1935:94; Swanton 1946:plate 89). By the 1870s, Seminole graves
in southern Florida had the appearance of small log houses and
were designated by the word *to-hop-ki*, meaning "stockade" or
"fort" (MacCauley 1887:521). Even the coffins used to bury the
Indians at Fort Brooke were called by them the "narrow house"
(Prince 1836:October 13 in Prince 1836–1842). Scaffold burial was

noted among the central Florida Seminoles by Dexter (in Boyd 1958) as late as 1822. Curiously, local tradition in the vicinity of Dade City describes the location of a scaffold burial ground in a heavily wooded hammock. Below-ground burials were still practiced by other Seminoles, although after 1818 guns and ammunition were no longer included as burial goods (Young 1934–1935:94). In this light, the clan plots at Fort Brooke exist in striking contrast to the individual treatment characteristic of earlier Seminole burial customs and do perhaps, as the Pipers suggest, signal the changes (stress) then being experienced by Seminole society.

Additional information about Seminole society of the 1830s may be gleaned from a consideration of the five burial groups at Fort Brooke (see figure 9 and table 5). The burial lots contain a mix of adults of both sexes and children (with the exception of Burial Group 2) and reflect the expected demographic sample as drawn from a larger population (see Wienker 1982). The burial groups probably did not represent family plots, because several of the groups contain subsets of individuals of approximately the same age—not to be expected in a nuclear family but a strong possibility if the sample was drawn from several related families. Clearly the Seminoles were fond of children; the quantities of personal ornaments found with child burials are striking indeed, especially in comparison with items buried with adults in the same group (however, see table 5; some adults were buried with goods). Yet other accounts relating to Seminole ethnohistory suggest the possibility that Seminole parents may simply have bestowed seemingly lavish wealth upon their children; some decades later MacCauley (1887:488) observed that mothers proudly dressed their infant daughters with strands of beads, and again we should recall that Philoki dressed his two young sons finely for a visit to Rolle's plantation in 1764. Beyond the fact that the Seminoles were genuinely fond of their children (MacCauley 1887:498; Spoehr 1941:21), children also provided them with additional means to display the wealth of their family, and we have already discussed the importance of displayed, or wearable, wealth to the Seminoles (see chapter 3). The emphasis on stature and wealth visually communicated through

Table 5. Burial Groups at the Fort Brooke Cemetery

Number	Sex	Age	Artifacts
			Burial group 1
53	female[a]	25–35	iron belt buckle, 5 U.S. Army brass buttons, 3 smaller buttons, 114 necklace beads
52	?	2–4	1 iron cup, 1 metal spoon, 3 button fragments, 1 brass bell, 814 necklace beads
31	?	5–7	2 iron cups, 6 perforated coins (1819–1822; 3 Spanish, 2 American, 1 British), 2 white metal earbobs, 1 metal bodice piece, 860 necklace beads
30	?	4–6	2 iron cups, 1 iron knife with copper case, 6 perforated coins (1821–1839, Spanish reales, U.S. dimes), 1 metal bodice piece, 1 earbob fragment, 2 brass button fragments, 102 necklace beads, 226 seed beads
29	?	1–3	19 necklace beads
			Burial group 2
19	?	2–4	3 cone-shaped white metal earbobs, 8 teardrop white metal ornaments, 456 necklace beads, 0.5 oz. seed beads
20	?	4–6	114 necklace beads
21	?	5–7	794 necklace beads
			Burial group 3
42	?	2–4	6 coins (5 two reales, 1 one real, 1777–1809), 235 necklace beads
45	?	6–8	39 necklace beads
43	?	2–4	1 brass door knob, 767 necklace beads
61	?	0.5–1.5	2 cone-shaped white metal earbobs, 2 perforated coins (Mexican ½ reales, 183?), 2 white metal bodice pieces, 839 glass necklace beads, 0.75 oz. seed beads

[a]Probable identity
Source: Piper and Piper 1982

Number	Sex	Age	Artifacts
63	?	17–25	2 pewter 4 hole buttons
44	male[a]	25–35	2.5 oz. white seed beads, below knees in diamond pattern

Burial group 4

Number	Sex	Age	Artifacts
60	?	2–4	2 metal cups, 1 knife, 168 necklace beads, 1 brass military decorations holder
62	?	2–4	1 white metal crescent gorget, 2 white metal pendants, 2 white metal bracelets, 2 cone-shaped earbobs, 187 necklace beads, 5 oz. white seed beads
77	?	9 mos. –3 yrs.	1 perforated coin (Spanish 2 reales, 1796), 1 knife with bone handle, 1 white metal bodice piece, 591 necklace beads
69	male[a]	17–25	none

Burial Group #5

Number	Sex	Age	Artifacts
100	?	4–6	3 iron spoons, 1 iron bowl, 2 iron cups, 1 iron handle, 1 knife with bone handle, 8 brass buttons, 9 bone, 15 pewter, 2 white metal arm bands, 1 white metal bodice piece, 1 white metal earbob, 2,021 necklace beads
111	male	adult	"pouch"; 1 iron arrowhead, bodice piece, gun flint, ramrod fragment, copper wire coil, 5 flat copper sheets, 1 whetstone
110	male	17–25	1 white metal earbob with cloth attached

costume was not likely to lessen in the turbulent atmosphere surrounding the Second Seminole War, and indeed portraits of Seminole warriors of the period show their concern with jewelry and elaborate garb (see Fundaburke 1958).

With respect to artifacts found with the burials, the coins of Spanish denomination minted before 1813 (Piper and Piper

1982:233–238) hold special interest and hint at previous Seminole commerce with the Spaniards. The blue-faceted glass necklace beads favored by the Seminoles are present in some quantity, and bead types found at the domestic site of Nicholson Grove (see chapter 4) are also included in the Fort Brooke assemblage. The diamond or diamondback motif that is so prominent in southeastern Indian decorative arts appears at Fort Brooke as a seed bead embroidery pattern on a woolen garter (Piper and Piper 1982:153, 223, 227) and resembles known ethnological specimens. But perhaps the most interesting aspect of the Fort Brooke collection, from a comparative perspective, is the way in which its entirely European- or American-derived items contrast with contemporaneous Seminole domestic assemblages known from excavations along the Withlacoochee River where few trade items have been recovered. This disparity between assemblages may have resulted partly from a conscious choice on the part of the Seminoles to reject the cultural values of dominant American society.

Nativism in the Withlacoochee Cove

With the signing by some of their members of the treaties of Payne's Landing and Fort Gibson, the Seminoles gave the United States the impression that they had relinquished their Florida holdings in favor of a reservation adjacent to new Creek lands in the present state of Oklahoma (Mahon 1967:76, 82). Had the Seminoles in fact left Florida en masse following the last of these treaties in 1833, there would of course have been no Second Seminole War (historians call Jackson's invasion of the peninsula in 1818 the First Seminole War). But while some bands did not need undue persuasion to accept the government's terms and leave the territory (for example, Charley Emathla, mentioned earlier, and Black Dirt, who lived in the vicinity of Chukochatty; Swanton 1928:394), other bands decided to resist efforts ro remove them.

Osceola, sometimes called Powell (the surname of Osceola's mother's husband; see Boyd 1955), had secluded himself and his followers in one of the most remote pockets of the Moultrie Creek reservation, the Withlacoochee River wetlands near the place where Sitarkey's Negroes had settled in about 1814 after the disbanding of the Alachua Seminoles. Beginning in November 1835, from his new stronghold deep in the fastness of the swamp, Osceola would orchestrate events that in swift succession were to bring him and his people into armed conflict with the U.S. Army and the militia of various states. On November 26, as previously noted, Osceola killed Charley Emathla on the road near Fort King because of Emathla's intent to emigrate. Three weeks later Osceola ventured north to Black Point, on the rim of the Alachua savanna, and there ambushed a baggage train laden with supplies (Mahon 1967:101). Twin strikes occurred on December 28, 1835, when Osceola and a band of warriors killed the Indian agent Wiley Thompson, his companion, and the post sutler outside the walls of Fort King. To the south, the Seminole chiefs Micanopy and Alligator, with Seminole blacks led by Abraham, dispatched Major Francis Dade and his command in a surprising hail of gunfire. Unaware of the Dade massacre but aware that the Seminole force of resistance was building to the south of the Withlacoochee River, General Duncan Clinch and volunteers led by Richard Keith Call moved against the northern flank of the Seminoles on December 31, 1835, in the Battle of the Withlacoochee (Mahon 1967:107–112; figure 10). The Second Seminole War had commenced.

The so-called Cove of the Withlacoochee (so named because the north-flowing Withlacoochee forms a big bend in this area) was a carefully chosen stronghold for the base of guerrilla operations in the opening years of the war. Its one hundred square miles of mixed hammock, swampland, and prairie were as unfamiliar to the Americans as they had been to the Spanish and British of earlier times; indeed, accurate maps of the area did not exist prior to 1837. Prehistoric Indians in the area were visited by the conquistador Hernando de Soto in May 1539 on his trek north and at that time were constituents of the aboriginal province known as Tocaste. Excavations under way at a burial mound attributed to these Indians suggest some aboriginal occupation in the area as late as the early 1500s (Mitchem and

Hutchinson 1986). The years between then and about 1814, when Sitarkey's blacks settled in the area, reflect a cultural hiatus, at least where the present state of knowledge is concerned.

Other factors besides desired seclusion influenced the Seminoles to settle in the Withlacoochee Cove and the Wahoo Swamp, just south and east of the Withlacoochee. The fact that Sitarkey's blacks had already pioneered the area and were producing crops was one advantage. In addition, the blacks would prove to be valuable allies in the hostilities ahead. It is also likely that a number of the Seminoles taking sanctuary in the Withlacoochee Cove, especially Osceola and the Tallassees, had some knowledge or memory of the Creek stand against Andrew Jackson at Horseshoe Bend, Alabama, in 1814. The prophet-directed construction of the warrior's village of Tohopeka in the bend of the Tallapoosa River bore in its geographical setting a remarkable similarity to Osceola's village and other Seminole settlements in the Cove (see map of Horseshoe Bend in Dickens 1979:2, 6, and compare figure 10). Tohopeka and Powell's Town (hereafter the term that I will use to refer to Osceola's Withlacoochee village) may both have had as their model the archetypal Creek town, described by Bartram: "An Indian town is generally so situated, as to be convenient for procuring game, secure from sudden invasion, having a district of arable land adjoining, or in its vicinity, if possible on an isthmus betwixt two waters, or where the doubling of a river forms a peninsula" (Bartram 1955:400). I will discuss other locational factors with respect to the archaeological site of Powell's Town in chapter 6. Spiritual reasons, that is, the influence of the prophets, should not be downplayed, despite their lack of success in stemming the American tide in Alabama. Initially at least, it seems to have made little difference to the followers of a prophet whether or not his powers could stand up to empirical, real-world tests (Nunez 1958).

Despite the documented importance of the Withlacoochee Cove with regard to Florida history, U.S. military history, and the culture history of the Seminoles, the locations of Osceola's village and other Seminole sites in the area remained archaeologically unknown until 1983. In May of that year, Florida State

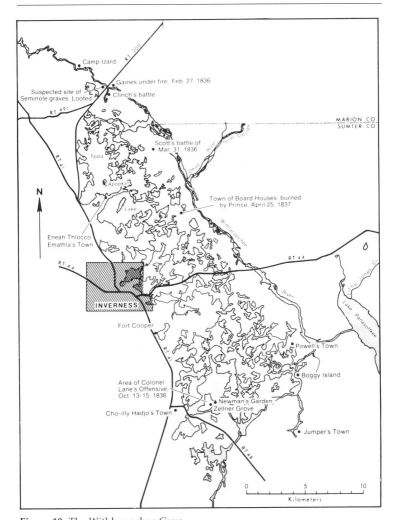

Figure 10. The Withlacoochee Cove

Museum archaeologist Jerald T. Milanich and I traveled to the Withlacoochèe Cove wetland east of present Inverness, carrying with us a diary penned by one Lt. Henry Prince of the U.S. Army. This diary contained passages and maps relating to his participation in the 1836, 1837, and 1842 campaigns waged against the Seminoles in this portion of Florida. The diary contained a short description and a sketch map of the Powell's Town site—enough, we thought, to enable us to relocate the site some 147 years after its abandonment by Osceola and his band. Because the Prince diary has proved to be a valuable new source of Seminole ethnohistory and has literally pointed the way to the archaeological discovery of several previously unknown Seminole sites, I will now discuss it at greater length.

The Prince Diary

The Prince diary was formerly in the possession of a Dr. Charles A. Van Slyke of St. Paul, Minnesota. The connection between Prince and Dr. Van Slyke is at present unknown. Upon his death in 1940, his daughter, the present Lucille Coggeshall of Altamonte Springs, Florida, took the diary with her to her residence in New Jersey, where she stored it until 1968. At that time, her husband, Ralph H. Coggeshall, at his wife's suggestion, unpacked the diary and on rainy days began the process of collating the pages. By 1979, Mr. Coggeshall had developed an interest in Second Seminole War history and took the manuscript with him on a visit to Florida. While visiting the Dade Battlefield Park, Mr. Coggeshall was given the name of the local Seminole war historian Frank Laumer. Coggeshall and Laumer met, and during a subsequent visit to New Jersey in 1980, Mr. Laumer arranged for the purchase of the Prince diary, eventually secured by the Wentworth Foundation, a private, nonprofit organization dedicated to sponsoring research and educational endeavors concerned with Florida history. Its president, William Goza, presented the diary on the behalf of the Wentworth Foundation to the P. K. Yonge Library of Florida History, Gainesville, where it remains at present. Mr. Laumer has recently provided a typed transcription of the diary, also available in the P. K. Yonge Library.

Henry Prince was born in Eastport, Maine, on June 19, 1811, and graduated from West Point in 1835. By January 1836, Prince was in Florida to fight in the Second Seminole War and received the first of his several war wounds shortly thereafter in the Izard battle fought on the banks of the Withlacoochee in late February and early March. In 1847, Prince was wounded again, this time at the Battle of Molino del Rey, in the Mexican War, and was disabled from these wounds until 1850. In the Civil War, Prince served as a brigadier general and was held as a prisoner for a time in 1862. In 1877 Prince was serving in the capacity of deputy paymaster general, a post from which he retired in 1879. On August 19, 1892, he ended his own life in a hotel in Trafalgar Square, London.

Prince's duty in the years 1836–1842 took him from Florida to Nassau to Kentucky. During these years he spent considerable time in the vicinity of the Withlacoochee Cove. He witnessed two pitched battles there against the Seminoles early in 1836 and returned in the spring of 1837 at the command of General Thomas Sydney Jesup to produce an accurate topographical map of the area for the general's files.

Throughout his diary, kept in a notebook that must have been similar to a modern surveyor's field book, there appear the flourishes of a poet. Consider its first line, on January 10, 1836—"Land of Flowers"—"aim to gather laurels," to his lamentation upon the death of Dade (1836:January 31)—"but Death belongs to the human family . . . what is it to die, to be shot in some vital part and suffer no more!" By February 17, Prince, stationed at Picolata, had learned of further combat—the Battle of the Withlacoochee (Clinch's offensive of December 31, 1835). Word in the camp was that "Powel," or Osceola (Prince used the idiosyncratic spelling of "Powel" throughout the diary), had been shot twice in that engagement but was recovering. On February 18, Prince marched to Fort King and there learned the story of Wiley Thompson's murder at the hands of Osceola from a Seminole black named Cudjo. According to Cudjo, sixty Seminole warriors had remained concealed in the scrub outside the fort for two days; finally, they "drew T.s spirit" so that he took a stroll in their direction and was subsequently shot down. While at Fort King, Prince learned that the fighting force of Seminoles had recently been joined by four hundred Creek warriors.

On February 26, 1836, Prince moved out to the Withlacoochee with General Edmund Gaines and soon had his first taste of action. Eight miles from Fort King, the troops passed a deserted Indian and "negro" town and, near the Withlacoochee, a burial ground. An abandoned town was burned where the command met the river, at a point several miles north of the present bridge on Route 200. They then traveled upstream (south), crossed the river for a time, and found the bodies of two of Clinch's casualties disinterred. By the next day they were themselves under fire from the Seminoles occupying positions on the west bank. By February 29, the army had stockaded itself behind a log breastwork, named Camp Izard ("Izzard" in Prince's spelling) in honor of Lt. James Izard, who fell in action at that place (see Mahon 1967:147). Prince himself was hit by two spent balls, one in the hip and one in the back. Gaines meanwhile lost his only tooth in a similar fashion. The Indians laid siege to Izard and set fire to the palmettos surrounding the army's position. For some reason a white man was among the Indians that day.

On March 1, a Seminole warrior killed by grapeshot was dragged into Camp Izard. According to Prince, he had in his possession a powder horn containing powder of the best quality, a leather haversack holding a large quantity of bullets, a supply of flints, and a pick brush and chain for servicing a musket. That night an Indian could be heard making a loud oration on the opposite bank, closing with the words *momis tah* (Smithsonian ethnologist William Sturtevant takes this to be a declaration in the Creek, or Muskogee, language, meaning "it is so"; Sturtevant, personal communication, August 10, 1986). On March 3, the troops were subject to an Indian ruse, as Seminoles dressed in blue army greatcoats, forage caps, trousers, and short blue jackets moved through the underbrush in disguise. Prince learned that Osceola had made a speech to the Seminoles on March 1 and had advised, "We can't do anything with them here [at Izard] boys but we'll give it to them when they cross the river" (Prince 1836–1842:March 4).

By March 5 the surrounded soldiers had prepared horse head soup and liked it. On March 6 Osceola, Jumper, and Alligator parleyed with the army and warned them not to cross the river.

After this meeting, Captain Hitchcock remarked of Osceola: "Powel is a very interesting man, small, handsome, of a melancholy cast and a little talkative[;] alluding to the death of Thompson he says he is satisfied and doesn't care what course now is taken by the rest of the Indians." The council was interrupted by the arrival of reinforcements at Izard, who, misinterpreting the Indian presence at the camp, hastily fired off a volley and killed a Seminole. With this blunder the Indians slipped away and with them any hopes for an early conclusion to the war. The Indian dead now numbered thirty-three.

On March 28, 1836, Prince again arrived at Camp Izard, this time under the command of General Winfield Scott. On March 30 the troops crossed the river and advanced beyond Clinch's battleground of December 31 and into an open prairie. Here they were fired upon by Seminoles concealed in a thick scrub. The soldiers moved on the scrub but failed to engage the Indians. On April 1 two abandoned Indian towns located in the northern reaches of Lake Tsala Apopka were burned, and Maj. Mark Anthony Cooper was left with three hundred men to establish a post in the vicinity (see Baker 1976 for an archaeological description of this site; figure 10) while the rest of the force swept south to Tampa Bay. On April 5, the command arrived at Fort Brooke at the head of Tampa Bay, after passing Colonel Lindsay's northernmost encampment (Mahon 1967:143) south of the present Floral City, where the men saw that the corpses of several soldiers had been disinterred. They also passed through, and burned, the old settlement of Chukochatty. In the subsequent months there were several other actions in the Withlacoochee Cove (most notably that of Colonel Lane in October), and on November 27 Prince wrote of having learned that the cove had been "thoroughly scoured, and that there were no Indians there."

Henry Prince returned to the Withlacoochee region early in 1837. On January 12, near the Wahoo Swamp (east of the Withlacoochee in the vicinity of the present Route 48 bridge) Prince encountered a party of "friendly" Creeks (Creek auxiliaries; see Thurman 1977) who had with them a recently captured "Tallassa" Indian. "Tallassa," "Tallasay," and "Tallahassee" are names used to refer to the division of the Seminoles that derived from or near the Creek town of Tallassee on the Tallapoosa River and who contributed the Muskogee- or Creek-speaking element of Seminoles who were later to congregate northwest of Lake Okeechobee, near the present Brighton Reservation (see Boyd 1955:251 for related discussion). Fortunately, Prince took some care to record his interviews with this man. Two hundred and fifty men and a number of women and children of his tribe, he claimed, were encamped in near-starvation conditions deep within a coastal swamp on "Clear-water Creek" (either Crystal River or the Homosassa). The previous winter they traded deer-skins for gunpowder with Captain Bunce, who operated a fish-ery near Tampa Bay but now had little powder remaining. Indian "bullets" (shot?) were commonly of their own manufac-ture. Besides his camp, there were two other villages on the creek, one inhabited by the "Choceochutties" (surely once affil-iated with Chukochatty) and the other by the "Euchees." The Seminole also knew the whereabouts of Powell and the Ne-groes, that group having retreated to the fastness of the Wahoo Swamp (probably Kettle Island, Sumter County). Powell, he claimed, was well provisioned with powder because he had re-cently confiscated six kegs from the army. This Indian had fought against Prince and the others when Gaines took position at Camp Izard; by his count the Seminole force consisted of three hundred Miccasukis (in Prince's spelling), ten Tallahas-sees, a great many Negroes, and an unknown number of Topekayligays.

Prince, and the Creek auxiliaries led by Jim Boy, went in search of the Clear-water village and on January 18 encountered two members of the Tallasay band (again in Prince's spelling), identified by the captive as "Ista-Jago" and "Woz-wocky." These men, driving a pack pony loaded down with jerked beef, were killed when they resisted capture. Prince reached the Clear-water camp on January 19 and took five women, six chil-dren, and nine blacks (three men, three women, and three chil-dren) captive. From these prisoners Prince elicited testimony regarding the Indian side of the Clinch, Gaines, and Scott cam-paigns in the Withlacoochee Cove. During the hostilities, Prince was told, the women and children were hidden in the depths of the Wahoo Swamp. Alligator was said to be "very selfish in getting plunder" (Prince 1837:January 21 in Prince 1836–1842) and had shown further impropriety by driving away with him to Peace Creek cattle that belonged to other tribes. Powell, however, was esteemed as "the most *gentlemanly Indian* in the nation—he don't take white folk's things—he never even has got a horse" (Prince 1837:January 21 in Prince 1836–1842). The Indians also complained that, since the death of the Mikasuki chief at Fort Drane (August 21, 1836; see Mahon 1967:177), there had been little unity or leadership among them. With the captives, Prince and the Creeks traveled south to Fort Brooke, passing the town of "Eu-faw Tustenuggy" (Chukochatty?) and the town that Black Dirt abandoned upon emigrating to Indian Territory. Prince recorded that the Eufala Indians were now mixed with the Tallasays and were called the "Topkaligay."

The record of Prince's next trip to the Withlacoochee, during the week of April 19, 1837, has provided the basis for the direct historic approach to Seminole archaeology in the Withlacoochee Cove, and is therefore of particular importance. On April 17, Prince was ordered to make a reconnaissance of the Withlacoochee from Fort Dade to Fort Clinch (virtually its entire run), with the purpose of producing an accurate map of the vicinity in the event that the army would have to mount yet another campaign. Prince was also to be on the watch for any signs of Indians along the river. By April 19, Lieutenants Prince, Brent, and Bowman, with their men and two mule-drawn wagons, had passed through Cho-illy Hadjo, or Crazy Deer's Foot, Town, at the south end of Lake Tsala Apopka near present Floral City (figure 11). The remains of this town were located in my 1984 archaeological site survey of the area (Weisman 1985b) and were recorded as site 8Ci214. Cho-illy Hadjo was said by Prince to be a "law maker," or constable, to the Tallasays, a political office created in Creek government by Alexander McGillivray after 1784 (Green 1980:51). Thus it is certain that Cho-illy Hadjo and his band were of previous Creek affiliation and had removed to Florida after 1784, most probably after the Creek War of 1814. The night of April 19, Prince and his party made Fort Cooper.

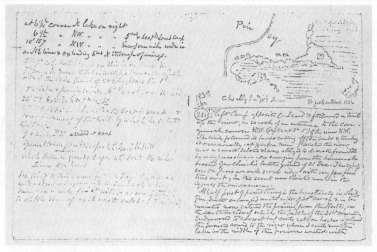

Figure 11. Cho-illy Hadjo's Town in the Prince diary

The following morning Prince attempted to reach the Withlacoochee by traveling back south to Cho-illy Hadjo's Town and
there turning to the east. He could not pass around Lake Tsala
Apopka, however, and doubled back to Fort Cooper. Prince
then moved out in the direction of Camp Izard, passing the vicinity of Eneah Thlockeo Emathla's Town (near the present
town of Hernando), which had been burned by Lt. William Fos-
ter's right-wing advance during Scott's offensive of April 1,
1836. Accompanying Prince was a black guide by the name of
Ansel, captured by the army in the "Pumpkin patch" on January 20, 1837 (Jesup 1837:May 8), who had been associated with
the Seminoles during their resistance in the Withlacoochee
Cove. Ansel had been with Osceola during Clinch's strike of December 31, 1835 (known to the Indians as the "battle of the spot-
ted lake"; Prince 1837:April 21 in Prince 1836–1842) and reported
that the Indian leader had been stunned when a cannonball
passed near him and was several days recovering. Osceola told
Ansel that, had Clinch not been turned back, his camp would
likely have been penetrated.

After two days at Fort Clinch, on the morning of April 24,

Prince, Ansel, Lieutenant Bowman, and seven mounted Georgia volunteers moved back south to explore the Withlacoochee Cove. Prince spent the night in an oak hammock due east of the present city of Inverness. On the morning of the twenty-fifth the party went in search of kindling for the breakfast fire. Soon it encountered an abandoned Indian town (near the site of the prehistoric Ruth Smith mound, 8Ci200), constructed of "Indian boards" (pine), which proved ideal for firebuilding. At least one house was dismantled for use as kindling. Beneath one of the houses was a bark-lined pit containing a powder keg made from green animal hide.

The next passage, combined with the accompanying sketch map, directly sparked the search for Powell's Town that led to the present book and I will cite it in full:

> At length we arrived at Powel's Town. Here Ansel was acquainted. He pointed out the field, the square, gave situation of the river and everything. All of which I found to be correct upon examination. Powel's Town is on a little oak scrub elevation in a very large opening. There are no trees in sight except those on the hammock islands and on the river—no pine. The cattle pens are built of hard wood. [Prince 1837:April 25 in Prince 1836–1842].

Across the Withlacoochee was Boggy (now Kettle) Island, where according to Prince (information he probably learned from Ansel) was a "hiding place but little known even amongst the Indians" (Prince 1837:April 25 in Prince 1836–1842). In the interior of the island was a field where the blacks would seclude themselves "in time of war." The nameless "negroes" of the Prince account were certainly Sitarkey's blacks, formerly from the Alachua savanna. Their settlement on the banks of the Withlacoochee, mentioned by Dexter in 1823, closely matches the location and description of Prince's Boggy Island.

After less than half an hour at the abandoned site of Powell's Town and after traveling to the banks of the river to view the approach to Boggy Island, Prince decided to strike a course back to Fort Cooper following his compass on a southwesterly bearing. The beeline route from Powell's Town to Fort Cooper (approximately seven air miles) was greatly complicated by the sloughs, swamps, and marshes of Lake Tsala Apopka (especially in the vicinity of what are today known as the Miley Islands, on the Flying Eagle Ranch), and by 4:30 in the afternoon the party found itself finally on dry land, to the south of its intended course and still some four miles from the fort. Here, above the southeast shore of Lake Tsala Apopka, the men came upon an abandoned Indian town of board houses, divided in two by a "perfectly black creek" and connected by a footbridge. Passing through this town they proceeded west until they were halted by the lake itself in the vicinity of Duval Island. Here Prince noted that thirty or forty green hides had been left on the shore by the Indians for use as boats. Ansel was then sent south to pick out a route skirting the lake, which he did, and by 6:30 P.M. the men had emerged on the Fort Cooper road, south of Cho-illy Hadjo's Town and five and one-half miles below the fort. Well after dark, his horse whinnying with delight at the site of Fort Cooper's lights, Prince, Ansel, and the Georgia Volunteers approached the safety of the fort's stockade. The Prince map (Prince 1837) filed with General Jesup the following month plotted the course of Prince's travels and illustrated the locations of abandoned Indian towns and fields in the Withlacoochee Cove.

Between May 1837 and May 1838, Prince traveled to Havana, Key West, and Nassau, then back to south Florida, where the Second Seminole War was now centered in the vicinity of Fish-eating Creek. During the latter part of May 1838 Prince scouted in the area of Payne's Prairie (he calls it by name), also Waca-hoota, Micanopy, and the Suwannee, where he held that "the spirit of Sam Jones [Arpeika] pervades these woods if perchance he is not here himself" (Prince 1838:May 18 in Prince 1836–1842). In June 1838 Prince was off to Savannah and in 1839 was dispatched to the Smoky Mountains, then Kentucky, and other points north.

Diary entries resume on April 5, 1842, when Prince was back at Fort Brooke. Here he was asked by Colonel Worth to compile his notes on the Withlacoochee, as part of the colonel's planned cleanup operations in the central peninsula (Mahon 1967:300). On April 11, 1842, Prince was again at Fort Cooper, the next day at Camp Izard, and the following day turning south to penetrate the Cove much as he had five years earlier. As Prince traveled overland through the Cove, Major William Belknap commanded a fleet of canoes upstream; both parties were looking for the few Indians who had heretofore managed to escape death or capture. Prince attempted to access Boggy Island, but when he was unable to do so, he and his men camped in a hammock known today as Princess Island and feasted on sour oranges (which can still be had at that location). The last entry in the diary was written on April 16, 1842, when Prince was on the Withlacoochee and Belknap was on Lake Panasoffkee awaiting further orders from Colonel Worth.

The archaeological value of the Prince diary is demonstrated by the location and excavation of Powell's Town and the "black creek" village in 1984–1986. In anthropological terms, the diary provides something of an insider's view of Seminole life during the Florida campaign because of the native testimony elicited and recorded by Prince. Furthermore, Prince's own observations can be interpreted for insights into the subjects of Seminole society, economy, politics, ethnicity, cosmology, strategy and tactics, and material culture.

It is clear from the account that, while the Seminoles acknowledged the authority of a few titular leaders (Micanopy for one), the nature of their real authority was neither coercive or unifying. The three major tribal or ethnic divisions of the Seminoles at the time consisted of the Tallassees (various spellings), evidently Upper Creek transplants from the vicinity of the Tallapoosa River (central Alabama), the Mikasukis (various spellings), presumably representing the earliest Seminole elements in the peninsula, including the Alachua and coastal bands plus groups that had formerly resided in the panhandle region, and the Topekayligays, a composite group also derived from Upper Creek migrants, with a range across the midportion of the peninsula from the present Pasco and Hernando counties east to Lake Tohopekaliga in Osceola County.

Cattle were valued as a dietary staple and as wealth on the hoof. To judge from the numbers of animals encountered by Prince and other chroniclers (see, for instance, Potter 1836:94),

the Seminoles delayed butchering their animals as long as possible, perhaps because they could be hedged for cash as Charley
Emathla had done. Jerked beef figured importantly in the Seminole diet, and attempts at agriculture were made. Supplies
were to be had by raiding, by capturing military stores, and
even, it appears, by trading with merchants in the vicinity of
Tampa Bay.

In the Indian world spiritual forces still prevailed. The
Thompson murder had been accomplished only after Thompson's spirit had been influenced to walk in the Indians' direction. The Withlacoochee Cove may have been perceived as
something of a "promised land"; the whites were repeatedly en-
joined not to cross the river, and the Indians took extreme of-
fense when the army felled the forest in the vicinity of Camp
Izard. For their part, the army realized that the Cove held allure
for the Seminoles and feared as late as 1842 a rebuilding of Indian forces in the area. The battles fought on the Withlacoochee
were of the greatest intensity of any in the seven-year war, and
the Seminoles early perfected the guerrilla techniques that
would on more than one occasion disable the enemy. The archaeological identification of Seminole battle positions may
yield interesting information about native concepts of the conduct of war (for an opposing view, see Fairbanks 1978:186). Further ethnoarchaeological implications of the Prince diary will
now be considered in greater detail.

Seminole Ceremony and Ritual
in the Withlacoochee Cove

A fortunate side effect of the Second Seminole War is that
there is an increase in narrative accounts that pertain to the Seminoles. Aspects of their customs, practices, and beliefs again at-
tain a visibility comparable to that which they enjoyed in
Bartram's day some sixty years earlier. Particularly in the realm
of religious practice, the Prince diary and other documents (see
also Sturtevant 1962) hint at the strong role that ritual played in

the lives of the Seminoles during this era. Indeed, this role might be expected, given the fact that current circumstances favored institutions that promoted ethnic identity and group solidarity. In the long run, the war ripped Seminole society apart less than it forged a strong sense of ethnic identity. Its effects were ultimately constructive, not destructive, when viewed from a cultural perspective. Furthermore, a study of Seminole ritual during the Second Seminole War emphasizes the importance of historical or antecedent institutions for the Seminole present and underscores the quality of cultural plurality that is fundamental to Seminole culture history. The following examples illustrate these points.

"Feu de joie"

On February 28, 1836, Prince was with General Gaines and his command on the east bank of the Withlacoochee at the site of Camp Izard. Gaines's intent was to push an offensive into the Indian heartland across the river, as Clinch had attempted to do on December 31. However, Gaines was pinned down by heavy Indian fire and had been forced, essentially, into a state of siege. On the night of February 27, Prince wrote that the Seminoles were heard to discharge a "feu de joie" (fire of joy) that he interpreted as some form of native celebration. The following day (February 28) the Indians again discharged their guns, and now Prince paid close attention (Prince 1836:February 28 in Prince 1836–1842):

> [A] party on the left gave a distant shout or scream—as soon as they stopped the tribe near our front gave a tremendous reply, of more pretentious to the effect than the little whi-yi—the first syllable was shrill long and glided down the octave, the second was a short loud bass gutteral sound simultaneously by the whole tribe as if struck from one prodigious instrument. The word appeared to be kirr-wowh! kirr-wowh! kirr-wowh! wowh! wowh! wowh! This ceremony was performed twice over—then both parties fired a rattling "feu-de-joie."

It is useful to compare this account to features of the so-called gun ceremony as it was practiced by several tribes throughout the historic Southeast. In the 1740s, the Coweta Creeks, upon the death of one of their fellows, would "immediately fire off several guns, by one, two, and three at a time, for fear of being plagued with the last troublesome neighbors [the souls of the departed]: all adjacent towns also on the occasion whoop and halloo all night; for they reckon, this offensive noise sends off the ghosts to their proper fixed place, till they return at some certain time, to repossess their beloved tract of land, and enjoy their territorial paradise" (Adair in Swanton 1928b:391). The use of guns in burial ritual persisted among the Creeks through the 1830s and was noted following their removal to Indian Territory (Swanton 1928b:393, 394). These groups may have also incorporated the firing of guns into their annual busk ceremony as a "gun dance" (Swanton 1928a:567, 587). Gun ceremonialism was also present among the Chickasaws (Swanton 1928a:512). A related association between the Withlacoochee ceremony and native death rites is found in the gutteral "wowh" repeated by the Seminoles, which resembles a sound in the death song of the southeastern Indians (Swanton 1928b:421).

Because the gun ceremony is not known for the Seminoles before Prince's account, it is possible that one of the Upper Creek groups migrating into the peninsula after about 1814 was responsible for its introduction. In fact, as late as February 1836 up to four hundred refugee Creek warriors took up with the Withlacoochee Seminoles. An unusual confirmation of this move comes from an account reported in the *Florida Herald* of May 12, 1836, which I cite in full:

A silver whistle was found on the banks of the Withlacoochy which was recognized to have belonged to a brother of Captain B—— more of the Columbia Volunteers and who had been lost in the Creek nation nearly a year since. The name of the owner was engraved at length upon it. This circumstance adds strength to the opinion which had been advanced on the breaking out of hostilities that an understanding exists between the Seminoles and the Creeks, and proves conclusively that some communication has been had between the two tribes.

Possibly, the feu de joie ceremony on the banks of the With-lacoochee was performed to drive off the souls of the slain, who now numbered as many as thirty-three (Prince 1836:March 11 in Prince 1836–1842). The burial site of these individuals has not been located, but several years ago it was reported that a number of shallow burials were removed from a spot near the Indian positions during the Izard siege (figure 10). Unfortunately, details of the looting, and looted goods, are not available.

The tribes involved in the Izard fight are identified in the Prince diary (1837:January 13 in Prince 1836–1842) as the Mikasukis, the Tallasays, and the Topkaligays. The latter two groups probably represent the latest Creek elements to join the Florida Seminoles and probably later combined to form the Cow Creek Seminoles (MacCauley 1887:508 recorded a "Tallahassee" clan among them), ancestors of the Brighton Seminoles of the present day. Indeed, among this group, a gun dance was witnessed in recent times as part of hunting rites (Capron 1953:186, 187). The transformation of the gun ceremony from a funeral practice to an element of busk and hunting ceremonialism may have been under way in the Creek area by the mid-1830s (see the account of John Howard Payne in Swanton 1932) and signaled the evolution of the Green Corn Dance as the symbolic nexus of both native religion and history.

Black Drink

The importance of the black drink in the social and religious realms of southeastern Indian life has been previously indicated. Its use reflected a concern with purity of mind, soul, and body. The drink was known among the Indians as the "white" drink, because the color white and the condition of purity were symbolically linked.

The black drink was drunk as a purification rite associated with the Green Corn Dance by the Seminoles of recent times (Capron 1953; Sturtevant 1954), but there are historical lacunae as to the form and function of its use through the course of Seminole culture history. The following account, written by W. P.

Rowles (1841), suggests an unusual association between the black drink and another male-oriented activity in the aboriginal Southeast, the taking of scalps. Rowles was a surgeon with the Creek volunteers under the command of Capt. J. F. Lane, who were part of General Call's strike against the heart of the Withlacoochee Cove on October 13–15, 1836. The troops swept through several villages before doubling back, so that "on returning to the towns there were found a large quantity of the herb from which they decoct their black drink, a number of recent scalps, and other appendages of a grand dance" (Rowles 1841:116). The Withlacoochee Seminoles took scalps from desire for prestige. Also it was thought that hanging enemy scalps on or near the residences of the deceased would placate the ire of their ghosts (Swanton 1928a:419, 424). It is difficult to determine any association between scalping and the black drink ritual based on ethnohistorical evidence. It is possible that a ceremony of this nature was the "scalp dance," about which Swanton tried but failed to gather information (Swanton 1928a:529). As with the gun ceremony, the Second Seminole War seemed to provide the Seminoles with the stimulus to develop new rites and recombine those gained through their cultural inheritance. Therefore, much of the symbolism associated with the medicine bundles of the recent Seminole busks (Capron 1953; Sturtevant 1954) harks back to the time when Seminole warriors stalked their military prey.

A more traditional use of the black drink as part of the Seminole busk is indicated by the excavated remains of what is being interpreted as a black drink pot from a site on the Flying Eagle Ranch (8Ci192) southeast of Inverness (Weisman 1983, 1986b:5, 7–9). Excavations at this site resulted from our first, and failed, attempt to locate the site of Powell's Town (it is, in fact approximately one mile south of the correct location), but we were successful in isolating what appears to be a Seminole component in a sand cap or mantle blanketing an earlier midden of the Weeden Island period. The stratigraphic definition and artifact associations of this site have been described elsewhere (Weisman 1986b), and I will only summarize them here. Sherds from a single vessel, a large globular jar with an orifice diameter of 30 cm, lightly brushed below the shoulder and with a punctated rim, were found buried to a depth of 10 cm in a layer of clean white sand that had quite clearly been added as a cap over the earlier prehistoric midden. In the same area were several sherds of green bottle glass (more were found in later testing around the periphery of the midden), some charred and broken deer bones, and large pieces of charred wood.

The site was regarded as the scene of a Seminole Green Corn Dance, an interpretation that is strengthened by Creek ethnohistory. At least by 1836, and possibly before, Creek busk festivities were sometimes held at some distance from the inhabited villages (to judge from a detailed firsthand narrative provided by John Howard Payne), in contrast to the earlier practice of holding the busk in a squareground town. The dance ground was prepared "with soil yet untrodden" (Payne's account in Swanton 1932:177), and new pottery vessels were manufactured exclusively for the occasion. These latter two practices emphasized the quality of purity associated with the rites. Although pottery making has been discontinued by the modern Seminoles, through the 1950s they continued to add a clean mantle of earth to the dance ground and to choose a secluded location (Capron 1953). The Flying Eagle Ranch site also meets these conditions, with its secluded location (the nearest village is at least one mile away), the mantle of clean sand, and the special black drink pot. In this case, the pot was made from a limestone-tempered paste (similar to the prehistoric type in the area known as Pasco Plain) and was presumably locally made. The rim punctations have their closest stylistic affinity with those on a Seminole vessel found near Lake Butler, Orange County (Goggin 1958:7A) and are not known from other pottery collections in the Cove, including the sixteenth-century Tatham burial mound. Thus it can inferred that the Seminoles used the site in the busk ceremony, probably dating to their occupation of the Cove during the 1830s. The settlement pattern that existed at that time, with dispersed villages connected by a ceremonial hub (see village locations in figure 10) persisted into recent times in the Seminole settlements in southern Florida (see Capron 1953:177).

Clan Camps: Seminole Domestic Groups in the Withlacoochee Cove

In aboriginal societies of the historic Southeast, the fundamental unit of interaction between an individual and society was the clan. Clans were composed of groups of related lineages, or descent groups, and provided for the organization of economic activities (land tenure and husbandry obligations), social customs (marriage proscriptions), warfare and the ball play, and political institutions (the offices associated with the town center). In the Creek area, the minimal geographical expression of the clan was the huti, or several neighboring households containing women related through a common, and real, female ancestor. In the process of Seminole culture history, the traditional Creek huti tended to segment from its affiliation with a town center, and finally the hutis themselves fissioned into nuclear families. In the era of the Second Seminole War, social conditions again favored clan bonds, and what is known as the Seminole clan camp developed (MacCauley 1887:507; Spoehr 1941:12, 14). The clan camp differed from the huti in that related women resided in the same household. All members of the camp were members of the same clan, except the married men, who belonged to the clan of their mothers. Clan camps were distinct geographical expressions of clan affiliation. Spoehr's map (1941:11) illustrates the organization of the Cow Creek camps as they existed in this century, with the Bird clan distributed in eight discrete camps, the Panther clan in six, the Talahasee (Tallahassee) in three, the Deer in two, and the Snake clan in one. The word *istihapo* denoted both the people and the place of the camp and expresses the same concept as the Creek *talwa*.

An entry in the Prince diary for January 19, 1837, suggests the demography of these camps during the Second Seminole War. On that date Prince captured a Tallassee settlement of five women, six children, and one man. In order to distinguish clan camps on archaeological grounds, material traits must be assumed to have been used by the Seminoles as clan insignia, which was in fact the case throughout the greater Southeast

(Swanton 1928b:235). Clan camps should form discrete, isolated cultural deposits. Also, because clan camps were taking form during the years of the Second Seminole War, their material culture should reflect processes of social adaptation then under way.

The Seminole sites in Newman's Garden (8Ci206) and the Zellner Grove (8Ci215) were located using the direct historic approach based on the Prince diary. The circumstances of their discovery and subsequent excavation have been presented elsewhere (Weisman 1986a, 1986b:15). The sites are attributable to the town divided by the "black creek," visited by Prince on the afternoon of April 25, 1837, on his way from Powell's Town to Fort Cooper (figure 12).

Four sites have been identified in the Zellner Grove (designated Zellner 1 through 4) and a single site in the backyard garden of Mr. and Mrs. Lloyd Newman. The Zellner sites are approximately 100 m apart and are presumably only a portion of the village that extended to the east to the vicinity of Newman's garden. If we assume the Zellner and Newman sites to be the west and east endpoints of the "black creek" village, its extent can be estimated at some 750 m.

The four Zellner sites were originally identified in surface collections of Chattahoochee Brushed pottery sherds, diagnostic of the presence of a Seminole site. Three of the sites were subsequently shovel tested and/or test trenched (1, 2, 4) in 10 cm arbitrary levels to a maximum depth of 30 cm, and the plow zone was determined to be approximately 20 cm thick in most cases. Artifacts attributable to the Seminole occupation of the grove were found in the upper two levels (0–20 cm), or within the modern plow zone. No significant subsurface distributions of artifacts were noticed, nor were any definite features identified, probably a result of repeated plowing of the field over a period of many years. Surface distributions of pottery (table 6) at the four sites were contained within areas of not more than 30 m in diameter, although artifacts were often found in clusters within this area. At Zellner 1, three such clusters were identified, but the cultural pattern they represent, if any, is not known.

Rimsherds were recovered from Zellner 1 and Zellner 2; a

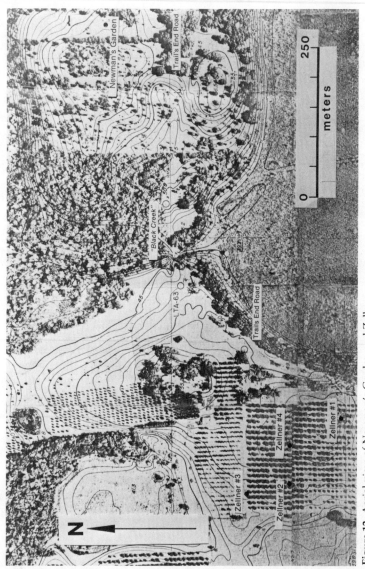

Figure 12. Aerial view of Newman's Garden and Zellner

Table 6. Artifacts from Zellner Grove

Zellner 1

Pottery (sherds/rims)		Shell	
Chattahoochee Brushed	27/1	Busycon fragment	1
Sand-tempered plain	19/0		
St. Johns Check Stamped	6/0	Lithics	
Pasco Plain	1/0	Flakes	31
Sarasota Incised	4/1	"Polished"	
		pebble	1
Glass sherds		Metal	
Clear glass marble	1	Lead shot	
Screw top lid		(spent)	1
(recent)	1	Iron strap	1
Clear glass		Military	
(recent)	1	"greatcoat"	
		button	1
Miscellaneous		Fauna	
Green glazed kaolin		Claw (mammal)	1
smoking pipe, fragments	2		
Fossil shark's tooth	1		
Rubber fragments (tire?)	2		
Shotgun shell (recent)	1		

Zellner 2

Pottery		Lithics	
Chattahoochee Brushed	54/2	Flakes	2

Zellner 3

Pottery		Lithics	
Chattahoochee Brushed	23/0	Flake (coral)	1
Sand-tempered plain	5/1	Flake (utilized)	1
St. Johns Check Stamped	2/0		

Zellner 4

Pottery		Metal	
Chattahoochee Brushed	68/0	Unidentified iron fragments	2
Sand-tempered plain			
(cazuela?)	15/2	Fauna	
St. Johns Check Stamped	2/0	Unidentified	1
Pasco Plain	2/0		

"fingernail" notched style from the former and a notched style from the latter (figure 13). These styles have also been identified in the historic Lamar series pottery from the Creek area (Dickens 1979:122, 128; also see Knight 1985 for discussion of Lamar). A small shoulder sherd from a cazuela bowl was found at Zellner 3.

Historic, nonaboriginal artifacts attributable to the Seminole were found only at Zellner 1. These were a military "Great Coat Button" (Wyckoff 1984:85) in use by the army between 1820 and about 1840 and found on early nineteenth-century military fort sites in Florida (Olsen and Campbell 1962:351; Clausen 1970:8–10), and portions of a green glazed kaolin smoking pipe, also dating to the early nineteenth century (Hume 1972:302; figure 14). No historic trade ceramics were found at any of the Zellner sites, a circumstance that also pertains to the Newman's collections. No items of personal adornment were recovered. In fact, the only Seminole bead (blue faceted) known from the entire Cove was found in Zone A of the prehistoric Tatham burial mound near the site of Powell's Town (but not, however, associated with any of the Tatham burials). There are also indications of a prehistoric component attributable to the Safety Harbor archaeological culture (circa A.D. 900–A.D. 1600) distributed lightly across the grove, and it is probably related to the more substantial Safety Harbor deposits on nearby Duval Island.

The wider variety of artifacts recovered in the Newman's Garden excavation (see table 7) indicates that the site was a cooking structure associated with the household complex (Weisman 1986a). The site was first identified on the basis of surface collections of Chattahoochee Brushed sherds, green bottle glass, and iron objects, all from within a dark soil stain measuring 31 m (N–S) × 17 m (E–W). Approximately 50 percent of the estimated site area was excavated in subsequent work (figure 15).

A single pottery rim style was associated with the site, of the notched fillet type also identified at the historic Creek component at Horseshoe Bend, Alabama (Dickens 1979:126). Sherds from several glass bottles were recovered, as were a number of metal items, including an iron fork similar to specimens recovered at Spalding's Lower Store (Lewis 1969:98; and in a pri-

Figure 13. Seminole rimsherds from Withlacoochee sites: A, from Newman's; B, from Zellner 2; C, from Zellner 1; D, from Flying Eagle Ranch

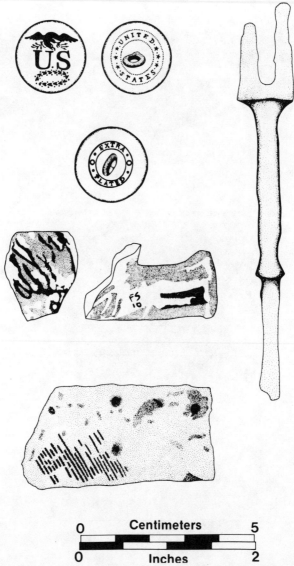

Figure 14. Selected artifacts from Newman and Zellner: top, buttons from both sites; right, fork, Newman; middle, pipe bowl and stem, Zellner; bottom, file, Newman

Table 7. Artifacts from Newman's Garden (8Ci206)

Pottery sherds/rims		*Glass (sherds/rims)*	
Chattahoochee Brushed	539/11	Green bottle	44/0
Sand-tempered plain	25/11	Black bottle	18/2
		White jar bottom, Letters "uine," recent	

Metal		*Fauna*	
		Unidentified fragments mammal(?)[a]	90
Flat iron file	1	Teeth	9
Nails	14	Phalanges	3
Wire	2	Rib (?)	1
Bail handle	3	Alligator scute	1
Iron tack	1	Snail shell	
Iron knife	1	(terrestrial,	
Lead shot		recent)	1
(.48 caliber)	1		
Cut brass	2		
Rolled brass	2		
Brass tack	1		
Brass button	1		
Snuff can			
(recent)	1		
Shotgun shell			
(recent)	1		
Steel shot			
(recent)	1		

[a]Probably a cow.

vate collection made at the site of Fort Brooke, established in 1824), a brass button possibly of military origin (Olsen 1963:553), a brass dome head tack of the sort commonly used to ornament gun stocks, luggage trunks, war clubs, or tomahawks (Lewis 1969:72; Piper and Piper 1982:253), an iron flat file, and a .48 caliber (11 mm) lead shot.

The reconstruction of the building that once stood at Newman's as well as reconstruction of those at the Zellner Grove is

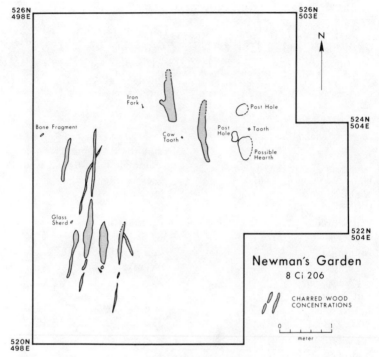

Figure 15. Site plan of Newman's Garden

facilitated by the account of W. P. Rowles, who, with the Creek
Volunteers commanded by Captain Lane, discovered several
Seminole towns in the vicinity (Rowles 1841:115):

> Within a short distance from the margin of the lagoon we entered
> a town, consisting of huts made by planting four forks in a quad-
> rangular form, over these poles were laid a roof of the bark (*Pinus
> mitis* and *P. strobus*, the *P. rigida* is also found) or boards split from
> the Pine or Castanea vesca, or American Chestnut. The walls
> were formed by bark or boards [the "board house" of the Prince
> diary] tied with splits or poles leaned against the evebeares. Fires
> were found burning and victuals cooking in several of the huts.

Together, the Zellner and Newman's sites present a picture of

Seminole domestic life and social organization at the beginning of the Second Seminole War. What were called towns by Prince and other observers were actually dispersed settlements of discrete households, or clan camps, whose women manufactured and/or used pottery with rim styles marking their clan identity. Because it is reasonable to suppose that the matrifocus of the clan camps would tend to concentrate material traits associated with female activities (in this case, pottery), not more than one decorated rim style occurs at each of the small domestic sites. Furthermore, the quantity of remains found at each of the sites suggests that they were used by a limited number of people for only a limited time. A town, or squareground, center probably did not exist at this time, with both the civic and sacred nucleus now being provided by the busk ground (the Flying Eagle Ranch?). This settlement pattern was observed for the Seminoles when they emerged again into ethnographic visibility near the end of the century (see MacCauley 1887).

Site inventories indicate that Seminole material culture was in part American derived (glass and metal) but that native pottery of traditional Creek form and style continued to serve important domestic needs (in fact, two intact Seminole vessels are known from isolated finds in the Cove, one a brushed jar owned privately and the other a plain cazuela bowl in collections curated at the Citrus County Historical Museum, Inverness). This pottery may have been viewed as a desirable marker of ethnic or tribal identity. Thus the reverse may have been true as well—trade ceramics were equated with the undesirable American presence. The colorful painted and transfer-print pearlwares that are so common on earlier Seminole sites (see the earlier discussions of Nicholson Grove, Paynestown, Mizell, and others as well as chapter 4) are simply not present in the Withlacoochee sites. It might be reasoned that the supply of these tablewares dried up with the onset of the war, but the Seminoles were able to obtain and use other nonaboriginal items, either through quasi-black market trading (for example, the activities of Captain Bunce; see Prince 1837:January 14 in Prince 1836–1842; and Mahon 1967:203), raiding, or trading with the fort-based sutlers through the end of 1835. Thus the absence of these goods from war-period assemblages may reflect purposeful exclusion. Comparison of Creek assemblages in Alabama offers supporting evidence. In the Tukabatchee area, trade ceramics were so common by the nineteenth century that "any native family would have possessed pearlware or whiteware plates, platters, saucers, serving bowls, and even teacups" (Knight 1985:180). This situation also existed among the Florida Seminoles, for instance at Nicholson Grove. Yet at the militant, prophet-directed Red Stick enclave at Horseshoe Bend (Tohopeka), where the resistance to Jackson and the Americans centered, these formerly ubiquitous ceramics are virtually absent (Dickens 1979:157). In the Creek region, the activities of known prophets (Tecumseh, Francis, and others) conformed to the described qualities of a nativistic movement (Wallace 1956), often founded to reject prevailing technological trends and to emphasize the value of the "old." At Tohopeka, in fact, directives issued by the Creek prophets were used to explain the nature of the archaeological record (Fairbanks 1962:48).

A similar phenomenon may have been occurring among the Seminoles in the Withlacoochee Cove. It was for a time the hotbed of the Indian resistance, the place where only those militant few who were determined to remain in Florida migrated and the place where the Indian military forces achieved their highest level of tactical organization. Many of the Seminoles who eventually resided in the Cove had previous experience with the Creek nativistic movements in the first decades of the 1800s. The appeal made by a Withlacoochee prophet would not have been strange. Unfortunately, this individual, if in fact he existed, has not been named in the documents. The one person who may have been able to exert such influence, Osceola, or Powell, will be discussed in the next chapter.

History records that the Withlacoochee Seminoles were not long able to remain in their desired homeland. Captain Lane's strike of October 13, 1836, moved to the core of the settlements and demonstrated their ultimate vulnerability. In fact, by the summer of 1836, Osceola had probably abandoned Powell's Town and after some time moved east of the river, to the area of the Boggy Island settlement of Seminole blacks. Within several months he was on the move to the St. Johns River and points east, where he was eventually taken into captivity on October 20, 1837. Other principals associated with the Withlacoochee resistance eventually surrendered or made their way south and east to the Kissimmee drainage and into the Everglades.

By 1840 a number of Seminoles had again sought out the Cove as a refuge, and minor military campaigns were organized in 1841 and 1842 to search for, and destroy, their villages. Military documents from these campaigns suggest an Indian lifeway remarkably similar to that which they adopted in southern Florida; small camps of three to four lodges hidden deep within the swamps, with their gardens located on nearby hammock islands (Clarke 1841). Some of these camps were used as stations to process what the documents refer to as coontie (most likely made from the root of *Smilax*), and others were used to turn beef into jerky. At one of these stations, the army destroyed an estimated twelve thousand pounds of jerked beef, abandoned on the lakeshore by fleeing Indians. The Seminoles themselves were not engaged by the military during this campaign, and they probably also slipped the noose and headed south.

The Seminoles were not, however, culturally vanquished by the events of the Second Seminole War. Many features of contemporary Seminole culture are the direct historical consequence of the cultural adaptations effected by the Seminole during this time. Such features include a renewed interest in Creek tradition and heritage, as evidenced in ceremony and material culture; the rebonding of clan ties; and an interest in assimilating plural interests and influences into their pattern of culture.

A Warrior and a Gentleman
The Archaeology of Powell's Town

The Seminole warrior known to history as Osceola, or Powell, has cast a shadow of legend and mystery unequaled by any other native American leader of the past or present. Part of the Osceola mystique lies in the tenor of the times; the Second Seminole War was as unpopular among certain factions of Americans then as the Vietnam conflict was in recent times. Indian sympathizers and a liberal press found in Osceola a heroic, and tragic, figure well suited to their aims. Furthermore, the enigmatic nature of the man—who would sit placidly for portraits painted by Catlin and others or would just as coolly plot the murders of his foes—made him at once knowable and unknowable, understood and misunderstood, and just the stuff of which legends are made. Consider the following passage, the oral testimony given by a fellow Seminole with regard to Osceola as recorded by Henry Prince (Prince 1837:January 21 in Prince 1836–1842): "Powel is a good warrior and a *gentlemanly Indian*. . . . the most gentlemanly Indian in the nation—he don't take white folk's things—he never has even got a horse. . . . he would be a good chief if he had the men—but alas! the Redsticks are but 8!" In the following account, published in the *Florida Herald* of January 13, 1836, Osceola's personality is given a slightly different assessment:

The Indian Chief Powell—the character of this chief is but little known, and not sufficiently appreciated. He is represented to be a savage of great tact, energy of character, and bold daring. The skill with which he has for a long time managed to frustrate the measures of our government for the removal of the Indians beyond the Mississippi entitle him to be considered as superior to Black Hawk. . . . [i]t is apprehended that he will give the Government much trouble and difficulty, if they do not act with decision and energy that becomes the power and the force of the country.

The personality of Osceola was riddled with contradiction, and he may intentionally have helped make it so. The view of him and his impact on Seminole culture history as derived from documents is as perplexing as the man himself. However, it is possible to write an archaeological biography of Osceola in which his personality becomes known through the study of material culture. These inferences are developed from recent archaeology at Powell's Town, the site of Osceola's Second Seminole War encampment in the Withlacoochee Cove. Indeed, the archaeology of Powell's Town cannot be fully interpreted without some knowledge of Osceola's personality and his role in Seminole society at the time of the Second Seminole War.

Osceola: A Brief Biography

The fullest nonfictional treatment of Osceola's life was published in 1955 (Boyd 1955, the primary source used below), while recent works have been concerned with the alleged looting of his grave site at Fort Moultrie National Monument on the night of January 7, 1966 (Dowd 1980), and the disposition of Osceola's personal effects after his death (Wickman 1986). Osceola's name upon birth, estimated from various sources to have occurred in about the year 1800, is not known; the name Osceola (derived from the Muskogee *Asi*, "black drink," and *Yaholo*, "singer" was probably conferred upon him in a naming ritual at the annual busk ceremony when he was initiated into manhood. *Yahola* was also the name of one of two Creek squareground deities (Swanton 1928a:485) who was entrusted with the sanctity of the grounds and its medicine. His parentage is a matter of some debate (hence the name "Powell," allegedly referring to his English father), but his mother is known to have been a Tallassee Creek and had, by 1818, become associated with the militant, anti-American Red Sticks, led by one Peter McQueen. McQueen was a targeted foe of Gen. Andrew Jackson and moved from the Creek area of southeastern Alabama to a settlement south of Tampa Bay to escape Jackson's retribution.

By 1821, the young Osceola and his mother had made their way to this settlement, probably near the present Peace River, where they joined a number of Mikasukis. After 1823, this band evidently made its way north to the vicinity of what would be Fort King, inside the reservation bounds specified in the Treaty of Moultrie Creek. The events of Osceola's early years promoted in him both a sense of tribal plurality—he was a Tallassee influenced by the Red Stick prophets and living with the Mikasukis—and a distinct enmity toward the Americans. He held no position of recognized tribal authority at this time, although he was known to the Indian Agents who, after 1827, were sent to reside at Fort King and monitor Indian activities on the reservation.

Osceola rose abruptly to power and prominence in October 1834, when his was the persuasive voice counseling the Indians not to comply with the government's wishes to have them emigrate. How Osceola's counsel gained legitimacy is not known, but he probably exhibited the skills of oration valued by the Indians. He also actively demonstrated his determination not to leave the peninsula. This determination was to set the course of his life for the next, and final, four years and would plunge the Seminoles into a conflict that would significantly mark their cultural identity.

By May 1835, Osceola and Indian agent General Wiley Thompson were in open conflict. In that month Osceola was clapped into irons for allegedly insulting the agent and thwarting his conciliatory efforts with the other Indians. Osceola and Thompson ostensibly resolved their differences, and the Indian was presented with a gift rifle as a token of goodwill. Osceola's pride, however, was probably not sufficiently soothed by this act and plans may well already have been afoot for revenge.

Yet Osceola was to consolidate his power not through an act of revenge but through the administration of what can be likened to tribal justice. In October 1835, the Indians met in the area then known as the Big Swamp, west of Fort King, and sealed a pact to execute any of their number seeking to emigrate. The pact was put to the test on November 26, 1835, when Osceola shot Charley Emathla (as late as 1938 the Seminole used similar means to dispatch persons who would not honor tribal law; see Capron 1953:197).

A similar fate was soon to befall agent Thompson, for on the late afternoon of December 28, he and several others were ambushed and killed outside the gates of Fort King. To judge from Cudjo's account (Prince 1836:February 18 in Prince 1836–1842), Osceola had now earned the authority to select "60 chosen tall Indians" to assist him in his plan to murder Thompson. This plan did not reach fruition, however, until the Indians "drew T.s spirit" and thus influenced him to stroll to where they lay hidden.

It is thought that Osceola masterminded the Thompson killing (it is clear that with sixty men he was prepared to attack Fort King if need be) and the near-simultaneous ambush of Major Francis Dade and his men on their march north to Fort King from Fort Brooke on the Fort King Road. If this is so, then the five months between November 1835 and March 1836 bracket the real zenith of his power. During this time he executed Charley Emathla, killed Wiley Thompson, plotted the Dade ambush, organized several raiding forays in the Alachua area, and was a principal in three Indian engagements with the military—against Duncan Clinch on December 31, 1835, against General Gaines in the Izard campaign of early March 1836, and in a skirmish against General Scott in the latter part of that month.

At this time, too, Osceola made his village at Powell's Town. After March 1836, Osceola's exact whereabouts are uncertain. In August of that year he, with three hundred Mikasukis, occupied the abandoned military post of Fort Drane, where he is thought to have contracted the malaria that would later prove to be fatal

(Boyd 1955:287, 288). Osceola was probably not in the immediate vicinity of Powell's Town when Captain (later Colonel) Lane's offensive nearly reached the site in October 1836, and by January 1837 he was rumored to be living with a band of blacks east of the Withlacoochee and south of Lake Panasoffkee (Porter 1943:408 in Prince 1836–1842), or in the area described by Prince (1837:April 25 in Prince 1836–1842) as Boggy Island. After August 1836, Osceola's immediate confederates may have dwindled to a mere eight, and these were Red Sticks. By the early summer of 1837 he had headed east to the St. Johns River, possibly hoping to rebuild his strength among the Mikasukis gathered there. There he was captured under the infamous white flag of truce on October 20, 1837, while attempting to parley with Gen. Thomas Sydney Jesup, commander of troops in the Florida campaign. The story of Osceola's capture and eventual death as a prisoner at Fort Moultrie, South Carolina, is told in Boyd (1955:295–299); the grisly circumstances and lore surrounding the decapitation of his corpse appear in Ward (1955) and Wickman (1986). Upon learning of Osceola's death, Micanopy, heir of the ancient Cowkeeper lineage and himself now awaiting deportation, remarked laconically, "Assin-ya-ho-la is dead" (Recollections of a Campaign in Florida 1845–1846:131). Osceola's power thus waxed and waned within the brief span of a year. His tribal authority was in demise well before his capture. The precipitous rise and rapid eclipse of Osceola's power was in part due to the Seminoles themselves and to his effectiveness in presenting himself as a leader worth following to the death. In the end, it was not the army that prevented him from succeeding but the Seminoles themselves.

Osceola's Leadership

The Seminole society described by Bartram in the 1770s had its civil authority vested in two offices. These were that of the town chief, usually of a white clan, who mediated town affairs, and the war leader, from a red clan, who coordinated warfare, raiding, and the ball game—all events that involved other bands or towns. As Seminole society gradually pulled apart during the periods of colonization and enterprise, the war leaders became increasingly dissociated from town affairs and roamed the Florida frontier for their own purposes. As the trend for downscaling accelerated, the power of the town chiefs eroded. A new order of authority developed, extremely local in scope and based on an individual's ability to provide for himself and his immediate kin in a trading economy. The net result of this process yielded the disastrous attempts by the U.S. government to find collective representation among the Seminoles with respect to land cessions and treaty regulations. This process was mirrored in the present century when the government again sought to deal with tribal representatives and ended up being forced to select their own (King 1978).

In the Creek area, different processes were in motion. Certain individuals had at times established some legitimate degree of tribal representation, for example the "Emperor" Brim in the early 1700s and Alexander McGillivray in the final decades of that century. During these years there developed a backlash in response to the rapid restructuring of Creek life that was occurring under increasing American influence. Indian Agents came to the Creeks nearly thirty years before their presence would be known among the Seminoles, and against their efforts self-declared "prophets" such as Tecumseh rallied their people to "throw aside the plow and the loom . . ., to use none of their arms and wear none of their clothes, but to dress in the skin of beasts" (Nunez 1958:7). The so-called Creek prophets attracted followers with their injunctions against the Americans, their supernatural abilities, and their use of magic, and by 1814 were associated with the Red Stick (a reference to the war bundle or war club) movement whose activities against pro-American Creeks provided Andrew Jackson with the motive and opportunity to move against them with military force.

The Red Stick movement also provided Osceola with the only model of political leadership he had known. He was not from a family of recognized leaders in Florida, nor did he establish himself with any notable degree of success. Indeed, traditional channels for men his age to gain prestige and wealth were not open to him under American rule. He had no power base in family, kin, or band support, other than the few Red Sticks with whom his mother had been associated. Therefore, his bid for leadership had to be predicated upon his ability to demonstrate legitimacy in the eyes of his fellows. He had to take steps to ensure that his authority was equated with what was good and right. In his mind this meant an emphasis on traditional, native-inspired values.

History provides several examples of the way in which Osceola manipulated the available material culture to enhance his image symbolically. There is the testimony of the "Tallasay" recorded by Prince (1837:January 21 in Prince 1836–1842) to the effect that Osceola was a "gentleman" for not taking "white folks' things." This is also the theme of the story of Osceola's victory over Catsha in a ball game organized near the post at Fort King. A quantity of goods had been wagered on the outcome by the commandant of the post, goods which the victorious Osceola deferred to the loser so as not to humiliate him. Instead Osceola is said to have claimed their equivalent in powder and lead.

Osceola sought power not in ostentation but through the ploy of humility, in the way of the prophets. That he was successful for a time is suggested by the domestic assemblages recovered from the Withlacoochee sites discussed in chapter 5. These sites had probably been occupied by Tallassees or Topekayligays, both groups derived from the same Upper Creek element as Osceola himself. It has been suggested that these groups experienced nativistic feelings and rejected American culture, evidenced archaeologically by the lack of imported ceramic tablewares at their sites. Osceola also developed some influence among the Mikasukis, whom he led in several engagements (*Florida Herald*, October 27, 1836; Boyd 1955:288). What factors led to his decline?

First, Osceola was simply unable to overcome the inertia of historical circumstance. The Seminoles had no precedent for consolidated, pan-tribal leadership, especially those individuals whose ancestors had been in Florida during Spanish and British rule. Second, the Seminoles were not as strong in their rejection of American culture and lifeways as were the Red Stick Creeks and were perhaps reluctant to follow an individual who acted like a Red Stick prophet (in the strictest anthropological sense, Osceola cannot be considered a true prophet because he is not known to have had a prophetic dream, or conversion experience; see Wallace 1956). One of the difficulties the prophets had in converting Indians to their aims was that the Indians had long become accustomed to the culture of trade and had based their own reckonings of prestige and wealth upon it. Thus the prophets misinterpreted the very nature of Indian history. For his part, Osceola, despite his machinations, ultimately remained an ambiguous figure in the eyes of the Indians—a warrior *and* a gentleman—and the most telling criticism of his leadership may be that the Seminoles simply did not know which lead to take. In a sense, his activities may have presaged the development of a new kind of social authority that would emerge in the next several decades, with the Seminole medicine men. Both civic and ceremonial responsibilites were entrusted in their hands. Ultimately, however, the Seminoles of the time were not willing to consolidate such trust with any one person, and leadership reverted to the level of the band. Furthermore, the confidence of the Indians in Osceola as a military leader may finally have been shaken by the fact that the army penetrated to the heart of his sanctuary by October 1836 (despite his threat that "we'll give it to them when they come over the river"; Prince 1836:March 4 in Prince 1836–1842), and that he was clearly in declining health soon after the failed attempt to hold Fort Drane.

The Archaeology of Powell's Town

The role of Osceola in Seminole society can be evaluated only in part through documentary means. In May 1983, the search for the site of Powell's Town began, organized by Jerald T. Milanich, of the Florida State Museum, William Goza, president of the Wentworth Foundation, and Donald Sheppard, a resident of Inverness. Identification of the Powell's Town site, if successful, might provide new archaeological perspectives on Osceola and the Seminoles during the Second Seminole War. The search was guided by the several pages of Lt. Henry Prince's diary (figure 16) that pertained to his discovery of the site in 1837, as recounted in the following passage (Prince 1837:April 25 in Prince 1836–1842): "At length we arrived at Powel's Town. Here Ansel was acquainted. He pointed out the field, the square, gave situation of the river and everything. All of which I found to be correct upon examination. Powel's Town is on a little oak scrub elevation in a very large opening. There are no trees in sight except those on the hammock islands—no pine. The cattle pens are built of hard wood." The first site identified on the basis of this description and the map shown in figure 16 was the Flying Eagle Ranch (8Ci192) midden, but the excavated remains and the negative results from systematic shovel testing in the surrounding hammock forced us to conclude that this was not the Powell's Town location (Weisman 1983, 1986b:7). We had erred in not following the diary description closely enough (Weisman 1987). The Flying Eagle Ranch site met some, but not all, of the conditions as recorded by Prince. Little attention had been given the fact that Prince placed Powell's Town on an elevated oak scrub. Given that Prince was very careful to record his natural surroundings and often distinguished between vegetative communities (hammock, slough, swamp, oak scrub, and the like), this specific reference to the habitat of the Powell's Town site was a crucial, and obvious, clue.

With funding secured from the Inverness Rotary Club, I spent the summer of 1983 conducting an archaeological site survey in Withlacoochee Cove (Weisman 1986b) and, in the evenings, compared the Prince descriptions of Powell's Town with modern aerial photographs of the area. By early August, I had combined all three lines of evidence contained in the diary—the bearings and distances of the survey log (which suggested that he traveled southeast to the river from Powell's Town, not northeast, as he had mentioned in the diary), the diary description, and the sketch map—to target an area known as Wild Hog Scrub, and asked permission of the property manager to field check my prediction. Wild Hog Scrub is indeed an oak scrub (meaning in this case the sand live oak) elevation, rising some ten feet above the surrounding prairies and river floodplain to

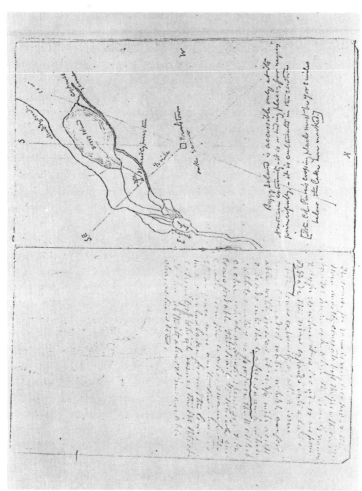

Figure 16. The Prince diary sketch of Powell's Town

the east, and is approximately one mile north (1,500 m) of the Flying Eagle Ranch midden. On our first visit to the candidate site, Paul Anderson and I and several volunteers surface collected several pieces of sand-tempered pottery, one piece of which was a rimsherd bearing Seminole-style punctations (figure 17). Unfortunately, the time for my return to Gainesville had come. We marked the location of our finds with survey tape and left until 1984.

In the summer of 1984, the site was again located, with some difficulty (the underbrush was and is extremely thick in the area), and additional surface finds were made. These included a sherd of dark green ("black") bottle glass, an iron bridle bit (figure 17), and, nearby, an iron kettle. That the site was Powell's Town was becoming more certain. In addition, the area gave all appearances of being undisturbed, and so the possibility of our finding significant artifacts and patterns of artifacts was judged to be good. With the assistance of a small group of volunteers, Anderson, Sheppard, and I fanned out through the dense scrub to continue our surface collecting and rather quickly came upon the site now known as the Tatham mound, a pristine burial mound of the Safety Harbor period that has, upon subsequent excavation, yielded Spanish artifacts dating, most likely, to the de Soto entrada, in association with aboriginal burials (Mitchem et al. 1985; Mitchem and Hutchinson 1986). Following the discovery of the Tatham mound and the suspected site of Powell's Town (both in Wild Hog Scrub, 800 feet [225 m] distant from each other; figure 18), trails were blazed in the vicinities of both sites, and plans were made to begin excavations in 1985. The initial excavations at Powell's Town, in March 1985, were supported by a benefactor of Citrus County archaeology and were conducted as part of a University of Florida archaeological field school under the overall direction of Dr. Milanich. The students spent one week at Powell's Town, and I spent an additional week there with the assistance of the Withlacoochee River Archaeology Council.

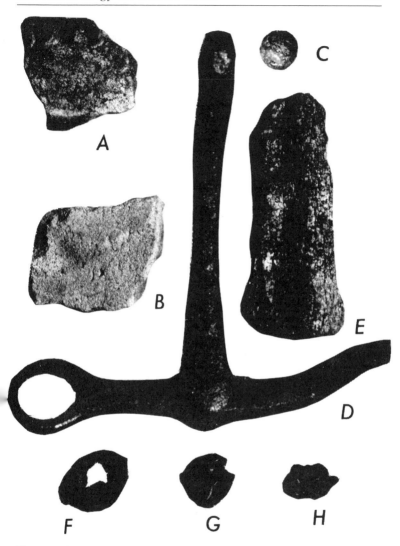

Figure 17. Seminole artifacts from Powell's Town: A–B, pottery; C, lead shot; D, iron bridle; E, cow bone; F–H, peach pits

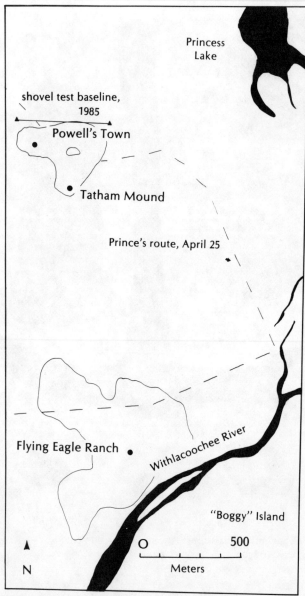

Figure 18. Location of Powell's Town

The 1985 Excavations

The objectives of the 1985 fieldwork were to define the limits of the Powell's Town site as indicated in the previous surface collections and to determine depths of the cultural deposits, the distribution of artifacts, and the presence or absence of subsurface features (hearths, trash pits, postholes) should we be successful in delimiting the site boundaries. To meet the first objective, a grid with intervals of 10 m was established to encompass all of Wild Hog Scrub (figure 19). The baseline was struck on the perimeter road on the north margin of the scrub, on an angle 95 degrees from magnetic north. The baseline was 480 m, east to west. Transects perpendicular to the baseline were created by turning a compass angle of 185 degrees and traveling south into the scrub. Crews of three to five members were dispatched into the scrub from baseline stations and were instructed to dig shovel tests of 50 cm × 50 cm (20 inches) at intervals spaced by 10 m (33 feet) to depths of at least 30 cm (12 inches) and to record stratigraphy and findings on a standard form. All excavated soil was sifted through screens with a one-quarter-inch mesh. In this manner, ninety-seven shovel tests were completed along seven transect lines spaced along 210 m of the baseline. Two of the excavated transects eventually intersected the Tatham mound at the southern periphery of the scrub.

The only artifacts found in the shovel tests were in the vicinity of the previously flagged surface finds, at the highest elevation of Wild Hog Scrub (figure 20). Pasco Plain (limestone-tempered) and sand-tempered plain pottery sherds were found here to depths of 30 cm, and while they did not provide any additional information about the Seminole component (being pottery types attributable to prehistoric Indians), their recovery did suggest that more substantive subsurface testing was warranted. Therefore, an east-west baseline was established with a transit and was staked out at intervals of 2 m, and a vertical benchmark was set in a nearby oak to provide a datum for vertical measurements. Seven units measuring 2 m × 2 m were excavated, in 20 cm arbitrary levels, and the soil (sand) was sifted through quarter-inch tripod-mounted shaker screens. Units were excavated to depths of 40 cm or 60 cm, depending on the vertical distri-

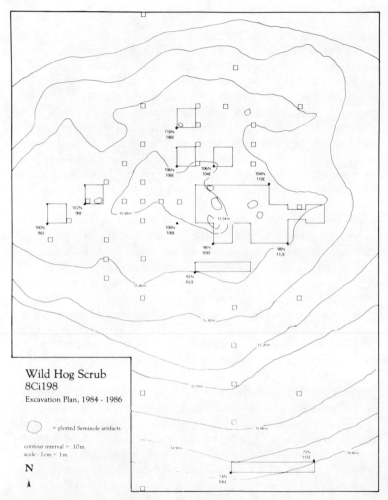

Figure 19. Excavation plan of Wild Hog Scrub

bution of artifacts. Results of the previous shovel tests indicated that stratigraphy could not be distinguished on the basis of natural zones, and this condition was quickly apparent in our larger 2 m block excavations. Below a variably shallow level of modern

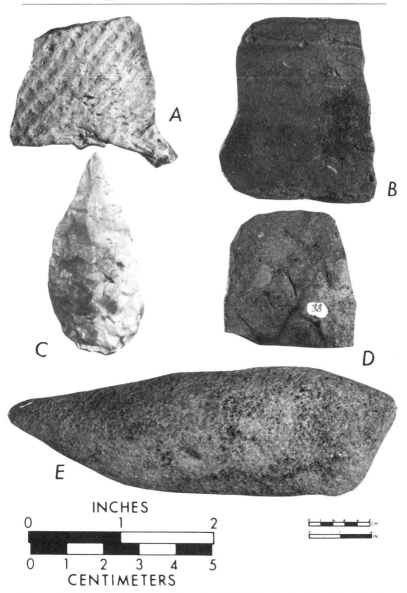

Figure 20. Selected prehistoric artifacts from Wild Hog Scrub: A, St. Johns Check Stamped pottery; B, sand-tempered plain; C–E, lithic tools.

Table 8. Historic artifacts from Powell's Town

Artifact	Unit	Level	Quantity
Glass			
Green bottle	100N/104E	0–20 cm	1
	110N/100E	surface	1
Metal			
Lead shot (.48 caliber)	100N/108E	0–20 cm (14 cm below surface)	1
Bridle bit	110N/106E	surface	1
Iron kettle	40N/244E (est.)	surface	1
Ceramics			
Stoneware sherd	102N/102E	0–10 cm	1

humus and leaf litter were deposits of up to 1 m of white fine to medium sand, underlain by yellow sands. No human-induced stratigraphy was observed—dark soil discoloration, midden staining, or the like—and no features were recorded. Worse, in our 1985 excavations at the site, we failed to realize until the end of our week that the site was multicomponent. Consequently, the arbitrary 20 cm levels in some cases obscured the true vertical relationship between the historic Seminole component at the site and those components attributable to earlier prehistoric occupations. Therefore, in several cases, bags of Level 1 artifacts, taken from 0–20 cm in depth, contained the pottery types St. Johns Check Stamped and Pasco Plain, known to be associated with late prehistoric peoples in the area, as well as plain, sand-tempered sherds of a compact, dense paste resembling that of known Seminole wares.

The 1985 excavations were successful, however, in providing additional archaeological evidence that the Powell's Town site had been used by the historic Seminoles. A sliver of green bottle glass and a lead shot were recovered in Level 1 (see table 8 for inventory), as were two peach pits and a cow bone, known food items of these Indians. The fact that these and other artifacts had been found in discrete clusters at the site, that is, some units contained artifacts, while adjacent units did not, suggested that further, and more refined, excavation might reveal the actual configuration of the Powell's Town site as observed by Henry Prince.

The 1986 Excavations

The Prince diary description of Powell's Town indicated that the site had a field, a square, and cattle pens. Did Osceola construct a square at Powell's Town, perhaps intending the site to be a traditional squareground town? Answering this question provided the primary objective of the 1986 fieldwork—to define the "square" in evidence at the site in 1837. A related goal was simply to recover more data relevant to Seminole material culture of the period. I returned to the site in September and, with the assistance of volunteer members of the Withlacoochee River Archaeology Council, gridded the entire site area surrounding the 1985 excavation at 2 m intervals. Systematic aligned 50 cm x 50 cm shovel tests were made along selected lines (figure 19). On the basis of the presence or absence of Seminole artifacts recovered in the shovel tests, judgments were made as to the locations of larger 2 m × 2 m block excavations. We hoped through this method to be able to determine where the square had been (relatively clean of artifacts), surrounded by up to four buildings (discrete clusters of artifacts).

Twenty-four shovel tests were excavated in the 1986 season, to an average depth of 54 cm. Approximately 83 percent of the tests yielded artifacts, meaning pottery sherds and lithic flakes or the occasional tool. Of the total, 35 percent of the tests contained sherds only, and 35 percent contained lithics only. Shovel tests containing both sherds and lithics tend to be located in the central portion of the site, within the 15.40 m contour line. Lithic materials have a broader distribution across the site and deeper provenance than does pottery. In the shovel tests, known or suspected prehistoric pottery types were recovered at depths of 37 cm (2), 35 cm, 34 cm, 28 cm, 27 cm, 25 cm, and 22 cm below the surface, or at an average depth of 26.8 cm. Pottery attributable to the historic Seminole occupation was found at 28 cm, 20 cm, 11 cm, 10 cm, 9 cm, 6 cm, and 5 cm below the surface, or with an average depth of 10.2 cm.

The pottery type Pasco Plain has the widest distribution and the deepest occurrence of any pottery type at the site and is, in fact, the most common pottery anywhere in the Withlacoochee Cove. Here it was found from approximately 16 cm to 61 cm below the surface. The type St. Johns Check Stamped, with a probable time range in this area coincident with the Safety Harbor archaeological culture (circa A.D. 900–1600), occurs at the site within a relatively narrow stratigraphic range, from approximately 20 cm to 30 cm below the surface. The above information suggests that the site has up to four cultural components. First, there is a low-density scatter relating to the historic Seminoles, from surface to 15 cm in depth. Below this is a Safety Harbor component to approximately 30 cm below the surface, underlain by another pottery-bearing (Pasco Plain) deposit attributable to Weeden Island–related peoples. The deepest component consists of lithic remains associated with an Archaic culture. This is a cultural stratigraphy supported by the vertical distribution of artifacts alone. Natural soil zones are not evident. No animal or plant remains were recovered from the suspected prehistoric levels, so that the function of the site for these earlier cultures remains in question. The recovery of the large stone grinding/digging tool (figure 20) suggests that the site may have seen some use as a seasonal foraging camp. Later, during the use span of the nearby Tatham mound (circa A.D. 1100–1600), the site may have served as a camp for people visiting or servicing the mound, although the precise nature of these activities is not known.

The Powell's Town Component

Because the Wild Hog Scrub site is multicomponent, I will designate as Powell's Town only that level which pertains to the alleged Osceola occupation of the site. Powell's Town contained a squareground, a nearby field, a cattle pen probably constructed of oak, and, by inference, the residences of Osceola and his followers. The program of shovel testing followed up by block excavations was intended to define these areas of the site (figure 19).

Eleven units measuring 2 m × 2 m were excavated during the 1986 season. Combined with the seven units dug in 1985, the total area sampled in the block excavations is 76 m². Shovel tests within the estimated area of the Seminole component total 4.25 m², making a total of 80.25 m² sampled within the Seminole area. As this latter area is estimated to include at least 240 m², 33.4 percent of it was sampled via combined shovel and block testing from 1985–1986. The maximum estimated site area, including the prehistoric deposits, includes some 600 m², thus the Seminole component, at less than a third of the total area and the most shallow of the cultural levels, rests like the tip of an iceberg on the Wild Hog Scrub site.

Archaeological evidence produced at Powell's Town suggests the existence of a square at the site, as defined by an area within the 15.50 m contour line (the highest portion of the site) that is virtually devoid of historic Seminole materials (figure 21). Shovel tests excavated within the area of the presumed square include 102/94, 102/96, 102/98, 104/96, and 106/102. Block units in the area are 100/102, 102/102, and portions of 102/104, 106/104, 106/100. Suggested dimensions of the square are 12 m east-west and 8 m north-south. The square is flanked by artifact clusters and/or surface finds attributable to the Seminole—on the north by the bridle bit and sherd of bottle glass, on the east by concentrations of pottery, the peach pits, bottle glass, and lead shot, and to the west by concentrations of pottery. Reasoning from the patterns of artifacts noted for squaregrounds elsewhere (Knight 1985:117), we can infer that the artifacts found at Powell's Town were once inside structures, other traces of which (postholes and hearths) do not remain. To the west of the squareground a single cow bone was recovered (Level 1 of the 1985 excavation, unit 100N/86E) that may indicate the location of the cattle pens, although subsequent excavations in the area did little to confirm this.

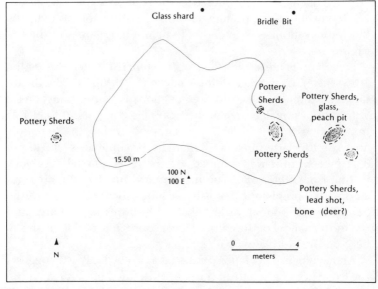

Figure 21. The probable square at Powell's Town

Powell's Town Artifacts

Table 8 reveals that historic artifacts at Powell's Town are decidedly scarce. They do, however, conform to our expectations
as to the types of artifacts likely to have been used by the Seminoles, and serve to confirm their presence at the site (figure 17).
Other nineteenth-century occupations at the site are unlikely on
historical grounds and in light of the scarcity of materials found.
The depauperate inventory of Powell's Town can be attributed
in part to the guerrillalike conditions of life and in part to the nature of Osceola's personality. After all, he was held in esteem by
his fellow Seminoles for not taking the white man's things, and
we have already discussed how this intentional poverty with respect to trade items may have enhanced his prestige in the
minds of his followers. Indeed, the quantity of historic materials
found at Powell's Town forms a striking contrast to the Seminole assemblages of Newman's Garden and Zellner Grove, dis-

cussed in chapter 5. Trade items in those sites, occupied for perhaps ten years before the founding of Powell's Town and abandoned shortly after the onset of the war, are relatively plentiful and, when compared with Powell's Town, suggest the bottleneck through which Seminole material culture passed between the years 1835 and 1836 (the spans of occupation are of course not comparable). Another contrast exists in the fact that, at Newman's, enough glass bottle sherds were recovered to permit almost total reconstruction of several bottles. At Powell's Town two glass sherds were found and one mere sliver (as was the piece of stoneware). Possibly items broken at Powell's Town were not discarded there but were instead reused, refashioned as bottle glass scrapers or other implements, or collected and discarded elsewhere (a practice recorded by Bartram for the Cuscowilla Seminoles).

The most common type of Seminole artifact at Powell's Town are pottery sherds ($n = 96$). Somewhat surprisingly, these are not sherds of Chattahoochee Brushed (present at Newman's and Zellner in some quantity) but are instead plain, with a dense, compact sand-tempered paste and burnished or smoothed surfaces. They resemble known plain Seminole wares (for instance, from Oven Hill) or, perhaps more closely, plain sherds of historic Creek pottery included in the Lamar series (Knight 1985:189, 200, 201; see also Dickens 1979:121). They can be distinguished from prehistoric sand-tempered sherds in the Withlacoochee Cove (found in area middens and the Tatham mound) on qualitative grounds—the compactness of the paste, the surface "burnishing" or smoothing, and their general hardness. They are not as burnished as specimens of the type Palatka Plain defined by Goggin (1958) from collections at Spalding's Lower Store. The single punctated rimsherd (figure 17) found is slightly outflaring and suggests a globular jar form common among Seminole pottery; a large bottom sherd indicates that one of the Powell's Town jars had a round bottom, similar to those on specimens known from Oven Hill. More detailed vessel form reconstructions are not possible, given the sample at hand. Clearly, however, native-made pottery was an important item of

Seminole material culture of the period, as here it was found in two of three suspected building areas at the site.

The intact cast iron cookpot found in our 1984 surface collection has been described in detail elsewhere (Weisman 1986b:14–16). Its manufacture dates to the British period in Florida, meaning that it had been in use for some time by the Seminoles before being discarded at Powell's Town. Actually, the pot was found a short distance to the east of the site, on a disused trail that may once have led from Powell's Town to a nearby spring or to the river. The bridle (figure 17) was probably not owned by Osceola, as he was said not to have a horse, but horses continued to be valued, prestigious possessions among many of the Seminole (hence it was odd that Osceola did not have one), and the bit may have belonged to someone else at his camp. Curiously, no items of personal adornment have yet been found, despite the fact that Osceola was portrayed in paintings just before his death wearing several strings of necklace beads, an embroidered sash, earrings, and other finery. It is possible that these items were obtained by him after his capture (it was noted in the Withlacoochee campaigns that he wore confiscated military dress; Mahon 1967:111; see also Prince 1836:March 1 in Prince 1836–1842) or were in the care of his two wives who may have been residing in the Wahoo Swamp during most of the hostilities. The recovery of the three (slightly charred) peach pits suggests that the Indians visited the sites of former Seminole plantations, likely those north and east of Tampa Bay, to obtain at least part of their produce. In sum, while the artifacts recovered and not recovered (for instance, lithics, beads, and pearlware) at Powell's Town allow some reconstruction of the activities that once went on there, they also provide an interesting look at the vanishing point of archaeological visibility. We are fortunate to know anything of a site occupied by as few as eight persons for a period of less than a year.

Osceola's presence at Powell's Town can be detected in three ways. First, there is the inventory of material items recovered at the site. This inventory is poor both in quantity and the range of artifact classes present. We know from a variety of sources that the Seminole did manage to retain a number of their possessions throughout the conflict (Sturtevant 1962; Piper and Piper 1982). They were not immediately reduced to a state of poverty by the circumstances of the war. Accounts also suggest that Osceola had a keen sense of the potential symbolic value of material items and manipulated them for his desired ends. He chose a path to authority that required him to divest himself of the trappings of the dominant American society and invest in the spiritual legacy of the native past.

Therefore, Powell's Town contained a squareground harking back to Creek and early Seminole tradition and perhaps the last of its kind built in Florida. While it is not possible to determine whether the square was constructed in the manner of the traditional town center (four cabins or roofed benches flanking an assembly ground) or as a domestic compound (up to four functionally distinct buildings relating to male and female daily activities, grouped around a square), in either case the use of space by Osceola was probably intentional, to express the fundamental principles that had previously ordered native life.

Osceola had to legitimize his power in the eyes of the other Seminoles. This concern is also reflected in the location of the Powell's Town site. Osceola hoped to make the Withlacoochee Cove the new Seminole homeland, and so Powell's Town, at its potential center, was located in the manner of the quintessential Creek village, "secure from sudden invasion, having a large district of excellent arable land adjoining, or in its vicinity, if possible an isthmus betwixt two waters, or where the doubling of a river forms a peninsula" (Bartram 1955:400). Powell's Town is located very near the Tatham mound (to date they are the only two sites identified in Wild Hog Scrub), and at the mound the only Seminole bead known thus far from the Cove was found, in Zone A, above the first level of prehistoric Indian burials. It is likely, then, that Osceola knew of the Tatham mound (it is only 200 m from the Powell's Town) and may have visited there upon occasion. Burial mounds were powerful and somewhat frightening locations to the Indians. Someone who purposefully sought out these locations would have possessed, in the Indian view, spiritual strength well beyond the ordinary. Osceola's purpose in locating near the mound may have been to increase his abilities as a warrior, by gaining this additional strength.

Osceola may also have strengthened his quest for legitimate warriorhood by locating his village atop a prehistoric Indian site, where in fact the most common (and perhaps most obvious) artifacts are waste flakes of chert. Chert and other small rocks figured prominently in the "power in war medicines" of the recent Seminole sacred medicine bundles, for example the *cho-no-thlee* described to Capron by a Seminole informant (Capron 1953:168): "you got to have *cho-no-thlee* in wartime or you can't win, . . . Osceola, he had that." If we assume that the modern medicine bundle specimens reflect some degree of historical reality (the way in which a crucifix symbolizes the crucifixion of Christ), the historical referent may be the sympathetic claim Osceola hoped to make on the lands of the Withlacoochee Cove by locating on a village site once inhabited by native Indians of the area. Therefore, the locational factors indicated at the Powell's Town site suggest Osceola's desire to fuse spiritual and secular powers into a new brand of Seminole leadership. His success rested on the fluency of the populace with their own past—would the symbols he invoked call forth from them the desired response? In the end, the Seminoles did not fathom the complexity of the man or the enigma that lay at his core.

Like Beads on a String
Observations on the Seminole Cosmos

For the few years between 1835 and 1838, Osceola tremendously influenced the direction of Seminole culture history. As with leaders of all times, Osceola's power resulted from a combination of charisma, historical circumstances, and popular perceptions as to the rightness or legitimacy of authority. Thus Osceola's leadership had a very personal dimension, determined in part by Osceola's own views about himself and his role in Seminole history and in part by the views held of him by other Seminoles. Cultures do not exist apart from the individuals who share a history and a society, and individuals do not exist apart from the configuration of self-images inherited by them from the history of their people. A full comprehension of the history of any culture can be gained only when it is understood how its people define themselves and how these self-definitions have changed or persisted through time.

Seminole ideas of selfhood were born from concepts within traditional southeastern Indian cosmology. Analysis of myth and ritual provides one approach for discerning the components of aboriginal selfhood. The focus of this chapter is on myth and ritual pertaining to the single-pole variant of the southeastern ball game. The limited evidence of archaeology, as combined with ethnohistory and aboriginal myths, suggests that the ball game had an important ritual context and may have originated in about A.D. 1000. The survival of the ball game among contem-

porary Seminoles suggests some continuity in beliefs and practices between these peoples and the southeastern cultures of
prehistory. Archaeological and documentary evidence indicates
that the ball game was in essence a ritual and thus served to en-
code and express messages about world view and the related
concept of selfhood (Fogelson 1971).

Notions of self and selfhood form matrixes through which
real-world experiences are filtered, and these notions create the
basis for behaviors through which individuals attempt to manipulate the social, political, and personal circumstances of their
lives to achieve desired outcomes. People bring an interpretation to the world around them. An interpretation of the world
that is shared by many people is called a "world view" (Ortiz
1972:137) and is one way in which societies distinguish themselves from one another. The components of a world view are
rarely made explicit but nonetheless exercise a very real influence upon a person's behavior, in the way in which language is
used without conscious reference to its rules of grammar.

The language of world view is symbolic. Cultural fluency is
determined by the extent to which this symbolic language is integrated into a person's self-identity. World view is a symbolic
model of reality, representing the limits of the "known world."
The behavioral correlates of world view are expressed on two
different levels. First, there are individuals, each moving
through the chartered autonomy of daily life. Next, there are individuals acting together, as one pulse in the social rhythm of
collective ritual. Collective ritual provides for the dramatic
expression of the moral imperatives meant to guide one's actions with respect to others and in relation to natural and supernatural forces of the cosmos. Collective ritual is successful
and will persist if the symbolic resources of its drama continue
to hold meaning for its participants. Because the symbols of ritual are historically constituted, because they are cultural products with historical referents often outside and well beyond the
experience of any living person, their full meaning cannot be re-
vealed in the absence of a historical perspective.

The Seminoles of the recent past, like nonliterate peoples
around the world, did not create textual histories full of people,

places, and events. History was alive for them, the past was made present, as at Osceola's squareground village of Powell's Town. History was embodied in the actions of living individuals or was expressed by the group through the drama of collective ritual. The most important of these rituals was the Seminole Green Corn Dance. The ball game had an essential role in the Seminole busk, because it presented a model of proper behavior with respect to one's fellows and to the world at large.

The Seminole Busk: Historical Concerns

The Seminole busk was an annual event timed to coincide with the first ripening of the young, or "green," corn. Green corn ceremonialism was a widespread cultural phenomenon in the aboriginal eastern woodlands (Witthoft 1949), and the Seminole version was unquestionably derived from the Creek *poskita* (Swanton 1928a:546), meaning "to fast" (Witthoft 1949:52). Ethnohistorical accounts of the Creek busk abound and together form a fairly complete picture of its practice throughout the lower Southeast for more than one hundred years (see Swanton 1928b for a thorough compilation). Although the Creek busk exhibited tribal, or regional, variation, certain elements were consistent in its practice. The busk ceremony took place in the ritually prepared talwa squareground, with civil and religious authorities both presiding. Its activities incorporated all members of society, and it had at its core a new fire ritual and a court day, or day of absolution. The ritual cycle lasted from four to eight days.

Unfortunately, the precise nature of the early Seminole busk is not known. Presumably early writers such as Rolle and Bartram were not present at the appropriate season or were not privy to this area of native life. British colonial documents hint at its presence (see Covington 1961:46), and brief mention is made of an "annual feast" among the Seminoles of Sanfalasco (near the present city of Gainesville) in the 1820s (Pierce 1825).[1] Full descriptions do not come until near the end of the nineteenth century (McCauley 1887:522; Cory 1896:16; Witthoft 1949:40).

From these descriptions and those of recent times (Spoehr 1941; Capron 1953; Sturtevant 1954), it is apparent that a considerable body of traditional Creek belief survived in the Seminole busk. After the Seminole wars, however, the Seminole ceremony revolved around the ritual display of the medicine bundles. The bundles are deerskin sacks containing the "Power of War" medicines and other sacra primarily concerned with war magic (Sturtevant 1954:36). The medicine bundles were under the care of medicine men, who would officiate at the annual busk, would unwrap and display the sacred objects, and would thus ensure the health of the tribe for another year. By the end of the Second Seminole War in 1842, the remaining Seminole in Florida were probably organized into groups or bands, each associated with one medicine bundle (Sturtevant 1954:42). The bundle, its keeper, and the dance grounds became the spiritual core of Seminole life, while the domestic seat was the matrilineal clan camp, or *istihapo* (Spoehr 1941:10). At the time of the annual Green Corn ceremony, these camps would, in Spoehr's terms (1941:16), draw together "like beads on a string," an apt simile as well for the role of the individual in Seminole society.

The Seminole Ball Game: Archaeology and Ethnohistory

Two types of ball games were played in the aboriginal Southeast. Their manner of play, the social contexts in which they existed, and creation myths regarding their origins appear quite distinct. Both have been classified as "recreational" activities (that is, non ritual) by ethnohistorians (Hudson 1976:408), which is, however, not quite the case. Pertinent here is the single-pole ball game, because of its ritual association with the Green Corn Dance. Swanton 1928b:456 and Hudson 1976:408, however, can be consulted for descriptions of the double-goal game. There are also wonderful depictions by Catlin of the game as played by the Choctaws (in Fundaburke 1958).

The single-pole game in the Southeast may have originated

with the development of the mound/plaza complex at the opening of the late prehistoric Mississippian period in about A.D. 900. Its appearance by A.D. 1000 is suggested by the excavation of a large post pit in the ceremonial precinct at Cemochechobee, in southern Georgia (Schnell, Knight, and Schnell 1981:34,35). Because Mississippian mound/plaza ceremonialism is the probable prototype for historic Creek busk and related practices, the early archaeological association between a presumed ball pole and a ceremonial precinct at this one site suggests a ritual context for the play of the ball.

The ethnohistory of the single-pole game further indicates its ritual nature, although among the Florida Seminoles its exclusive association with the Green Corn Dance did not occur perhaps until the mid or late nineteenth century. In very recent years, the game has been played for tourists and as a part of tribal social events. The single-pole game was first described among the Timucua of the northern Florida by LeMoyne in 1565 (Lorant 1946:107). This activity was unlike the later Creek and Seminole game in that it was played exclusively by young men. However, the ritual care given to the erection and decoration of the ball post (adorned with a string of beads, with a skin or tanned hide, and with a wooden frame or target on top) is, in its essential features, preserved up to the present by the Seminoles. The next account is provided in the testimony of the Franciscan priest Juan de Paiva, who in 1676 recorded a ball game myth as told him by an Apalachee chief, in which similar features of the ball post are explained on mythical grounds. I will give a version of this myth later in this chapter.

Later, the account of Adair from among the historic tribes of the lower Southeast suggests the ceremonial role held by the ball game by the 1740s:

> They assemble three nights previous to their annual feast of love; on the fourth night they eat together. During the intermediate space, the young men and women dance in circles from evening till morning. The men masque their faces with large pieces of gourds of different shapes and hieroglyphic paintings. Some of them fix a pair of young buffalo horns to their head; others the

tail, behind. When the dance and their time is expired, the men turn out a hunting, and bring in sufficient quantity of venison, for the feast of renewing their love, and confirming their friendship with each other. The women dress it, and bring the best they have along with it, which a few springs past, was only a variety of Esau's small red acorn pottage, as their crops had failed. When they have eaten together, they fix in the ground a large pole with a bush at the top, over which they throw a ball (Adair 1986:119; also see Swanton 1928a:551).

Hitchcock wrote a fuller description of the game, capturing the rush of action, after observing the Creeks in 1842:

The players mingle, or scatter about as they please, the men on one side and the women on the other aided by a few men. The men use sticks, the women their hands. The chief throws the ball up nearly vertically, standing near the pole—the game has commenced. All rush to sieze the ball, men and women pell mell together. One gets it. His party trys to give him an opportunity of throwing it. The opposite party, to embarrass him, rush on him, catch his arm, and in the whirl he loses the ball. Another rush. A woman gets it. She holds it firmly in one hand and walks towards the pole followed and surrounded by men and women. She is about to throw it. A ball stick is interposed over her. She sees one of her own side a little way off and tosses the ball to her. [Hitchcock 1930:157–158]

A form of the single-pole game is played among the postremoval Creeks of Oklahoma. In this game, men and women are still pitted against each other, the game was played in the squareground, and the pole was still treated with great care, now being decorated at the top with various carved animal images (Swanton 1928b:467; 1928a:544, 545).

The single-pole game among the Seminoles is known until recent times. A game played by them during the Garfish Festival in January 1986 near the Big Cypress reservation was remarkably similar to the game described by Hitchcock and can be traced to the game played formerly during the Green Corn Dance (Capron 1953). However, the first mentions of the ball game among the Seminoles clearly refer to the double-goal variety "brother of war" (Swanton 1928b:459), in which entire moieties or towns clashed (Bartram 1955:173; Rolle 1977:52).

In the early nineteenth century, a large game once occurred with more than one hundred Seminoles from the north peninsula present at the Okahumpka settlement of Micanopy (Boyd 1958:93). In 1836 the ballstick allegedly belonging to Micanopy himself was recovered when the U.S. Army raided the abandoned site of Pilaklikaha, where blacks associated with Micanopy lived, south of Okahumpka (Cohen 1836:176). Osceola was also a ball player of some skill, and trade goods were wagered on his performance.

It is likely that the single-pole game was present among the Seminoles before and during this period but was not observed. It is also likely that, after the Second Seminole War, the game came to be a part of the Green Corn Dance, as that ceremony came to embody combined Seminole beliefs about the cosmos. During this same period, accounts of the double-goal game disappear. Writing in 1896 on the basis of ten years' experience with the Seminoles, Charles Barney Cory indicated that the ball game was played on the afternoon of the first day of festivities, in this instance at a location in the Big Cypress Swamp. Some years later, Skinner (1913:76) pictured two wooden ballsticks, carved like wooden spoons, from another camp. The first full account of this position of the ball game with respect to the ritual round of the Green Corn Dance came in the 1953 publication of Louis Capron: "On one side, just outside the [dance] circle is the ball game pole—ko-ka (ball) a-pee (pole) (Miccosukee). This is a tall pine sapling 20 to 25 feet high, trimmed of branches but with the plume left at top. From about 4 to about 5 feet from the ground, this pole is squared and smoothed and on the flat sides score is kept with a piece of charcoal" (Capron 1953:182).

According to Capron, the game was played at sunset (or on the afternoon of court day), between males and females, using a deerskin ball stuffed with deer hair. The use of a ball of this type appears to be the most constant feature of ball games throughout the native Southeast. The males must use rackets, in this case constructed of green laurel (presumably *Ilex* spp.) bent over at the end so that a webbing of rawhide could be attached, while the females use their hands. To score, a player struck the pole with the ball in the designated place. After the game was finished, "helpers" to the medicine man in charge of the Green Corn Dance swept the dance track clean. The ball play was the first and only occasion in which women were allowed on the dance track, where the Green Corn ceremony would take place (Capron 1953:183). Thus the ball game took place next to the sacred stage on which the most important ritual event in the lives of the Indians was enacted. What meaning did the ball game hold in the symbolic expression of Seminole world view?

We may approach the cultural meaning of the Seminole ball game drawing on two different lines of evidence. First, the historical threads of ball game symbolism can be explored through an analysis of a myth purported to account for its origins among the Indians. In this way the elemental theme of the myth may be seen to provide the basic orientation for the Seminole world view as well. Second, the role and position of the game within the broader ceremonial round of the Green Corn Dance can be examined.

The Ball Game Myth

There are evidently no surviving myths among the contemporary Seminoles that account for the origins of the ball game. Several ball game myths collected among the Creeks by Swanton (1928b:55, 157) related to the double-goal game and quite clearly establish its importance in the red/white and war/peace dichotomies in Creek society. A myth relating to the single-pole game is provided in the account of Father Juan de Paiva, mentioned earlier, that was collected among the Apalachee and Yustega Indians in 1676. The Apalachee were soon to be exterminated with the collapse of the Florida missions at the hands of allied Creek and English forces. The cultural continuity between the events described by Paiva and the historic practices of the Creeks and Seminoles are clear. Translated versions of the myth (encumbered with the title "Origin and Beginning of the Ball Game which the Apalachee and Yustaga Indians have been playing from Pagan Times up to the Year 1676'') appear in several places. The short version presented here follows Bushnell:

> When the Apalachee nation was still heathen and living in darkness there were two caciques who lived beside each other, and their names were Ochuna Nicoguadca and Ytonanslac ("which are the names of demons," interjects Paiva). Ytonanslac had a granddaughter named Nicotaijula whom the principales of the place sent everyday to get water. While doing this errand she conceived and bore a son and hid him in the green plants. The Panther, the Bear and the Bluejay found the babe and took him to his great-grandfather, who made them promise to tell no one. The child was given the name Chita, and at the age twelve Oclati (Water Boy), and at age twenty, Eslatiayupi (Woman of the Sun). He was more skillful than anyone else with the bow and arrows and at the game of quicio which all of these nations play.
>
> Now it had been foretold to Ochuna Nicoguadca that he would be killed and his name taken by a son of Nicotaijula, and in case Eslatiayupi were her son, he wanted to kill him first. So he sent the youth three tasks: to get flints from the bed of a great river, to bring canes for arrows from a canebrake full of deadly serpents, and to take fledgling eagles out of a nest. Each time Eslatiayupi went to his great-grandfather for advice, and he was told to give a string of snailshell beads to a little bird who would get him the flints, to throw hoops of grapevine to distract the serpents, and to protect his head and hands with dried gourds and kill the eagles with a cudgel. At length Ochuna Nicoguadca, finding that he could not get rid of the young man in these ways, invented the playing of pelota [ball game] and that is where it came from [Bushnell 1978:10]

What does this myth tell us about the Seminole world view? First, the allegory that is the myth must be assumed to have some historical referent. It is not fiction but is in some sense real. Analysis of the myth is like that of a dream, only slightly less complex than the myth itself—symbolically robust, multiscalar, an expression of a people for whom past and present, history and culture, were not distinct dimensions of experience.

In the broadest sense, the myth stands as an allegory for the process of cultural dependence upon the growth of cultivated plants, while on the level of analogy the myth recapitulates in human terms the life cycle of plants (the growth of the boy is a metaphor for the growth of plants). In direct enthnographic terms, the periodic renaming of males as they progress through life stages known for the southeastern Indians (see Spoehr 1941:15 for a Seminole example) is clearly indicated. Known attributes of described ball poles also seem to have mythical precedent, especially the spray of branches and the eagle carvings mounted atop the pole, which may represent the nest of eagles mentioned in the myth.

The focus here is on the behaviors of the principals as described in the ball game myth, for these behaviors were meant to serve as a descriptive model for an individual's actions with regard to his own life and in society at large. If Chita is taken to be an Indian "Everyman," the meaning of selfhood is clear. Life is essentially the struggle to balance opposing forces in the world (figure 22). Figure 22 is a diagram of the ways in which benevolent and hostile actions of humans and animals influenced the actions of Chita, as told in the myth. One can, however, triumph through skillful individual action, as a boy becomes a man. This process was embodied in the life of every Indian male and was expressed repeatedly in the Indians' intercourse with the whites. They saw in the white man's enterprises opportunities to be, in effect, better Indians, through the demonstration of their personal skills (which, to judge from traders' and travelers' narratives, involved a considerable degree of personal danger). This self-identity pervaded early Seminole culture and would ultimately make its coexistence with the American impossible. It was not a "clash of cultures" that led to the Seminole's demise but a sameness in the Seminole definition of self and that of the Americans. Both stressed performance and competition, yet the same geographical bounds and resources were at stake.

The ball game, in myth and action, stresses triumph over adversity, but it holds another lesson as well. The reason is that the Seminoles did not exist in isolation but were, like beads on a string, drawn together into celebrations of group identity.

Figure 22. Schematic of the ball game myth

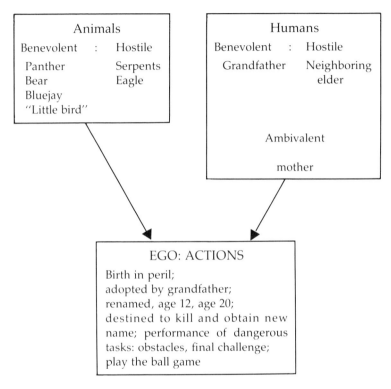

Thus the ball game was not an isolated activity but took place as a scheduled event in the Green Corn ceremony.

According to the primary testimony of Capron (1953:188–205), the Seminole Green Corn Dance was usually held on the fourth, and final, day of the festivities. Preparations for Court Day were under the strict guidance of the medicine man. He directed the preparation of the three black drinks to be consumed by the men and boys in the course of the day and night, and under his supervision the sacred medicine bundle was brought from its hiding place to the dance ground to be opened for inspection. The health and safety of the medicine bundle, which contained numerous individually wrapped sacred charms (like the cho-no-thlee, or "power in war," stones mentioned in chapter 6) and palladia, and the health and safety of the tribe were considered to be one. As the medicine lived, so the tribe would live. Its display at the dance ground signaled that all was well. Court Day would commence with the new dawn.

The first events of Court Day, once the medicine bundle was on display, included the feather dance, an intricate display of male solidarity in which all dancers carry staffs adorned with white bird feathers, and scratching, the ritual bleeding believed to promote a state of spiritual and bodily purity. Following these two activities, the first two black drinks were consumed.

At noon the council was held. Any man guilty of a crime against society since the time of the last Green Corn Dance could now atone for his actions before the elders, the medicine man, and other males representing all clans. The guilty party could admit himself back into the good graces of society by following the council of the medicine man, offered at this time, and by drinking a black drink. However, tensions could also mount by this time because it was not always assured that the guilty person would come forth or would desist from wrongdoing (in extreme cases, such persons were executed after repeated offenses). It is clear that the group preferred to have the slate wiped clean at this time, and to allow the strayed person back into their midst without further ado.

Until this time, the activities emphasized male solidarity and were the primary ritual vehicle through which male bonding was accomplished. Especially during the council of Court Day, males were encouraged to subsume their individual identities for the good of the group. Therefore, the tempo and mood of the proceedings stood in startling contrast to the ball play, which commenced just after the Court Day council and was held on the dance ground itself. Women were, for the first time, admitted to the dance grounds and formed teams that were pitted against the men in the wild play described earlier. The ball game did more than just relieve the somber atmosphere thus far prevailing over the ceremony, because it brought together two of the primary oppositions in native life—male and female—and encouraged the display of individual talents and abilities. Unlike the dance rituals of the ceremony, the outcome of the ball game was not certain, and it became like a drama.

After the game was over, the dance ground was raked clean by the medicine man's assistants and was ritually prepared for the climax of the event, the Green Corn Dance. Again, the emphasis was on group identity, but now the women were allowed back on the dance ground, where they appeared dressed in all their finery and wearing leg rattles. The dance itself began after midnight, after the men had imbibed the third black drink, and took place around the sacred medicine fire placed atop the clean sand at the center of the dance circle.

Thus is the climax of the single most important ritual of the year. In its pulse the ceremony alternated between emphases on the individual and on the group. The value of both was effectively presented throughout the course of the ritual, where they existed in a dynamic tension. In its entirety, the Seminole Green Corn Dance modeled the Seminole cosmos, in which the suggested limits of both individual and group action were presented. To the Seminoles, the message was clear, although perhaps expressed in the subliminal language of symbols. They are indeed like beads on a string, drawn together with other beads only once a year and in the main left to conduct life on their own.

The ball game was a significant feature of the Seminole Green Corn ceremony because it was valued by society as an important form of self-expression. The cultural meaning of the ball game can be approached through myth, in which the personal attributes of the mythic figure are presented as a model for individual behavior. The antiquity of the ball game myth cannot be determined, but the ball game was probably an element of the ceremonial complex of the late prehistoric Mississippian peoples of the Southeast. This ceremonial complex contained rituals associated with the chief/priests, warriors, and rites of agricultural fertility and hunting magic presumably associated with the commoners. There are suggestions that the single-pole ball game was originally featured as an element of one of the latter two activities, the prototypes for the busk and hunting ceremonies of the historic tribes of the Southeast. Whatever its early association, the ball game became a component of the Seminole busk probably by the mid-1800s and in combination with the other activities of the dance cycle that emphasized group solidarity, formed a complete descriptive model of the Seminole world view.

Seminole Studies
Topical Concerns and Directions

My consideration of Florida Seminole culture history began with the ancestral Creek pattern, the paradigm of cultural form and process from which historic Seminole culture developed. The ancestral Creek pattern is an archetype of Seminole culture history but not in the sense of a static collection of attributes and cultural traits. The ancestral Creek pattern is not a trait list but instead represents the interaction of cultural institutions, human volition, and historical circumstance.

In order to evaluate the influence of the ancestral Creek pattern on the evolution of Seminole culture, I sought to determine as closely as possible the elements of the pattern that were embodied in the founding populations of Seminoles. To that end I examined archaeological data and historical sources that pertained to prehistoric and early historic aboriginal populations in the Southeast, and I suggested that the Florida Seminoles were cultural heirs to trends that emphasized individual autonomy and selective acculturation. Contrary to the previous studies suggesting that the Seminoles depended on trade goods and therefore possessed a culture of less integrity than their prehistoric forebears, I established that the Seminoles had an active hand in shaping the nature of the colonial southeastern frontier, were cognizant of opportunities presented by the European eagerness for commerce, exploited those opportunities to full advantage, and all the while were successful in retaining a cultural

core that embodied fundamental beliefs and practices of the aboriginal southeastern Indians.

The Seminoles were also successful in absorbing a variety of
cultural influences over a relatively long period of time. Their
ritual and world view, as combined with threads of symbolism
and cosmology rooted in the late prehistoric Mississippian chiefdoms, forms a patchwork that is not immediately understandable on the basis of strictly synchronic perspective. I also
suggested that the Seminoles had a certain historical awareness,
although not in the Western sense of place and time, and that
Osceola and other key individuals in native American society
sought to manipulate symbols, or configurations of symbols, to
resonate with core beliefs held by the Indians. Perhaps Osceola's time, the Second Seminole War, was, more than any other
period in their history, the cultural watershed from which much
of the contemporary Seminole culture and personality has
sprung.

One of my goals in writing this book was to produce a culture
history in which the social, political, and economic conditions
that the Seminoles actually experienced were given full view, in
order that their active role in transforming their past and setting
the stage for their own present could be appreciated. This Seminole history is more than a curious appendage to the story of
southeastern prehistory and, at the same time, is a history
somewhat independent of historical sources. Critics may argue
that its interpretations exceed the data at hand, but I hope that
others will return to the subject and will improve upon its data
and interpretations. Indeed, it would be a fine state of affairs if
new lines of evidence could be developed to refute or confirm
various points that have here been raised. Seminole archaeology
is still in its infancy. There remain significant geographical areas
in which crucial events in Seminole culture history have occurred that are in need of archaeological exploration. Three
areas that may hold critical new information about Seminole culture history are the Wahoo Swamp, in Sumter County, where
there was a large village of Seminole women and children hidden away during the peak of the Second Seminole War hostilities in 1836, the upper St. Johns River, where there was a

substantial stronghold of Seminoles during that same war led by Philip, and the Kissimmee River drainage, one likely conduit for the Seminole migration into southern Florida in the middle decades of the 1800s. A definitive culture history of the Florida Seminoles will be possible only when these, and other, areas have been assessed through archaeological means.

However, future research may address an even more complicated situation. In 1957, the Seminole Tribe of Indians was granted legal status as a federally recognized tribe. However, its membership was drawn primarily from populations living in the Big Cypress Swamp, the area northwest of Lake Okeechobee, and near the Atlantic coast in what is now Hollywood. Many families living in or near the Everglades (now Everglades National Park) and west almost to Naples on the Gulf coast did not join the Seminole Tribe at that time but in 1961 gained federal status as the Miccosukee Tribe of Indians and were granted a small (338-acre) reservation near the Forty Mile Bend on the Tamiami Trail (U.S. Route 41). Later, the state of Florida granted the Miccosukees additional acreage adjacent to the Seminole reservation at Big Cypress, which is used primarily for hunting and fishing. Even before the legal formation of the tribe, the Miccosukees began plans to write their own tribal history (see Sturtevant 1971:120, 121; and King 1978), but as of November 1986 this project had not reached completion. In conversations with Tsani Yonah, a journalist hired by the Miccosukees to produce the textual history, I learned that the history had been a pet project of an administration now out of favor and that it is likely to languish, at least in its present form, under the new leadership. The information gathered by Mr. Yonah led him to conclude that the Miccosukees are a product of the combination of the Sawokli and Chiaha bands (Swanton 1946:116, 179), Creek tribes of the lower Chattahoochee drainage. This position is not significantly different from that presented by Swanton forty years ago. It is indeed likely that an association between the Miccosukees and one or more Creek tribes can be established on ethnohistorical grounds. Yet the question remains—are the Mikasukis of ethnohistory ancestral to the Miccosukees of today? Does archaeology hold the potential for enriching the tribal histories of contemporary native American polities in Florida? Conversely, is it likely that these groups can validate their claims to distinct tribal identity by archaeological means?

Tribalism and the Seminole Archaeological Record

Archaeological determinations of ethnicity or tribalism rest on the investigator's ability to demonstrate that the observed variation in the archaeological record through time and across space is attributable to the use of material culture by societies to create social boundaries. The ethnohistorical record can greatly enhance the determination of ethnicity by determining whether or not different tribal groups were in existence at a given time and what the nature of their interaction was. In the absence of ethnohistorical accounts, the investigator must prove strict contemporaneity between components of different archaeological sites, a task that is only rarely possible, given the almost inevitable limitations of archaeological data gathering.

However, documents and ethnoarchaeological studies are also useful in amplifying the social conditions that generate material culture variability. Examples are plentiful both in accounts and in studies of cases in which tribal or ethnic identity and configurations of material culture are not isomorphic. One instance is provided in the study of small-scale African societies by Hodder (1982:26–31, 35), which found that, when neighboring pastoralist groups were in competition for limited resources of land, tribal identities were clearly expressed through material means to justify situations of negative reciprocity or even hostility symbolically. In Hodder's view, similarities and differences in material culture are not simply a factor of ethnicity but are related to the circumstances of interaction between two or more groups.

Conditions of competition or hostility could also produce cultural similarities, as indicated by the following account of the Creek Indians provided by Bartram: "Some of their most favorite songs and dances they have from their enemies, the Choctaws; for it seems these people are very eminent for poetry and music; every town amongst them strives to excel each other in composing new songs for dances; and by custom amongst them, they must have at least one new song, for exhibition, at every annual busk" (Bartram 1955:326). Thus the Choctaw, although the enemies of the Creeks, had an active, ongoing, and creative role in the nature of Creek culture (the Choctaw-Creek enmity was preserved in a Seminole folktale of recent times; see Evans 1978:481).

Seminole archaeological remains vary across time and space. Ethnohistory tells us that the word "Seminole" was an umbrella term used to denote at least three distinct tribes, which during the Second Seminole War were called the Mikasukis, Tallassees, and Topekayligays. To what degree is the variability in the Seminole archaeological record attributable to the ethnicity of these three (or more) groups?

An examination can be made of the differences between the Oven Hill and A-296 sites, occupied during the colonial period of Seminole history. At Oven Hill, pottery rim styles exhibited a range of variation, vessel forms were diverse and specimens numerous, and a limited number of trade goods were present, including some that were likely associated with sociopolitical status. At A-296, however, rim style variation was minimal, pottery vessels few, and trade goods nearly absent. The two sites belonged to very different types, however. Oven Hill was very likely the squareground town visited by Rolle in 1764, while A-296 was an outlying family farmstead associated with Latchaway or Cuscowilla. Latchaway and the town on the Suwannee (Oven Hill) were by the mid-1700s still weakly linked through the system of intertown ritual and ball play that had been a feature of Creek life, and it is likely, though unconfirmed, that the Seminole towns shared some degree of tribal affiliation in their Creek homeland. Unfortunately, the Oven Hill remains cannot be compared to those of the "sister" site (Latchaway) on the Alachua prairie because that site is yet undiscovered. Nonetheless, the observed differences between Oven Hill and A-296 possibly reflect the different social and economic conditions then being experienced by the Seminoles, that is, life in the center or on the fringes, and do not express ethnic differences between the Alachua and Suwannee Seminoles.

The Seminole archaeological record through time also exhibits variations, demonstrated in the contrast between sites of the enterprise period (1767–1821) such as Nicholson Grove, Payne's Town, and Mizell, and those in the Withlacoochee Cove attributable to the Seminoles of the Second Seminole War era. The social conditions of these two periods, however, were so drastically different as to suggest that the simplest explanation for variability in the assemblages relates to the process of cultural adaptation. Furthermore, it is almost certain on ethnohistoric grounds that at least some of the Seminole population of the Withlacoochee Cove was derived from previously prosperous populations located in the highlands north and east of Tampa Bay. These were the Upper Creek Muskogee-speaking elements mentioned, most notably by Prince (1837), as the "Tallasays" and Topekayligays, using terms apparently provided by the Indians themselves. Archaeological sites associated with either or both of these groups have been identified in the southern portion of the Withlacoochee Cove, south of Lake Tsala Apopka and east of Floral City. The most characteristic features of these deposits are the presence of Chattahoochee Brushed pottery, identical to specimens of that type described for the Creek region, and the occasional recovery of military-derived artifacts in Seminole domestic contexts. The settlement pattern was a loose nucleation of clan camps, determined archaeologically by the discrete distributions of artifacts, each identified with a single style of pottery rim decoration. Rim styles may have become markers of clan identity as clan membership grew in importance after the mid-1820s. Pottery making at this time was still an important female activity (Pierce 1825). Thus the observed variation in material culture between domestic sites in the Withlacoochee Cove reflects social processes acting on the level of clan, not tribe.

The Prince document and other sources indicate that there were also numerous Mikasukis in the Withlacoochee area with whom Osceola was occasionally associated. The locations of the Mikasuki villages are not known but, if found and excavated, are likely to yield useful comparative data with respect to those sites located south of Lake Tsala Apopka. It was originally hoped that the excavations at Powell's Town would make it possible to determine the ethnicity of its residents, but in conclusion the site is better understood as the material expression of Osceola's personality and his short-lived quest for sociopolitical legitimacy.

The archaeology of Powell's Town emphasizes how an individual can be a source of considerable variation in the material culture record. Another example is provided by an eyewitness drawing of a group of Seminole men performing a dance in 1838 (Sturtevant 1962) near the St. Johns River. The drawing, done by Hamilton Wilcox Merrill of the Second Dragoons, depicts a dance group of eleven men circling around a fire. The leader of the dance has his arms outstretched, is bare headed, and is evidently chanting or singing (this is dancer number ten in Sturtevant's designation). Two of the men are unclothed except for breechclouts, while others are dressed in several styles of the Seminole hunting coat, or "long shirt." Several men wear patterned (probably beaded) garters, while the others do not. Four men wear plumed headdresses, one appears to be wearing a turban, two are depicted wearing crescentic gorgets (silver), and two wear earrings. These items appear to be typical of the day, to judge from various portraits and drawings reproduced in Fundaburke (1958) and from the archaeological assemblage recovered from the cemetery at Fort Brooke (Piper and Piper 1982). On the outskirts of the dance circle are two naked infants, a naked juvenile, and three other young men dressed in the long shirt. The individuality of all the participants is clearly expressed—all are identifiable as "Seminole," yet no person is dressed exactly like any other. Do the differences reflect ethnicity (in this case it is possible that all were Mikasuki, based on historical references; see Sturtevant 1962:75), personal preference and/or position, or clan? The fact that these questions can be raised suggests the complexity of the issue and the difficulty of finding an answer.

With regard to Miccosukee (the spelling of the modern tribe) archaeology, individuals of all three ethnohistoric tribes—Mikasuki, Tallassee, and Topekayligay—must be assumed to have survived in Florida through the Second and Third Seminole wars (the latter a guerrilla action between the military and the Seminoles in the years 1855–1858) to become the founding populations of the present Seminole and Miccosukee tribes, because the languages spoken by the Indians of the nineteenth-century—Mikasuki and Muskogee—are still spoken today. The Seminoles of the Brighton Reservation west of Lake Okeechobee speak Muskogee, while the Seminoles of the Big Cypress and Hollywood reservations and the Miccosukees of the Tamiami Trail speak Mikasuki. Thus members of the modern Seminole Tribe are almost certainly descended from members of the three ethnohistorically known tribes, while the Miccosukees are derived only from some part of the tribe that was formerly known as the Mikasuki. The relationship between ethnohistoric tribes and contemporary populations is most clearly expressed with the Brighton Seminoles, descendants of the Cow Creek Seminole of MacCauley's time (1887), who at that time had among them a "Tallahassee" clan, surely the Tallassees of history. Their route into southern Florida, along with the Topekayligays, may have been along the Kissimmee River, as is possibly attested by the isolated recoveries of several intact Chattahoochee Brushed vessels on that river as far south as central Okeechobee County (Goggin 1953:16). The identification of additional sites containing brushed pottery in the vicinities of Catfish Lake, Fisheating Creek, and Cow Creek (known locations of Muskogee-speaking camps from the 1870s through the 1940s) would provide the needed confirmation of this migration, but such sites have yet to be recorded. Pottery probably ceased to be manufactured in the 1840s and had become an antiquated practice for the Seminoles by MacCauley's day (1887:516).

The Miccosukee case is less clear. There are at least three possible source populations for the modern tribe, although all may be ultimately traceable to the Chattahoochee, Apalachicola, and Florida panhandle bands of the eighteenth century. First, the St. Johns River was a major haven for the Mikasuki, most notably under the leadership of Philip and Coacoochee (Wild Cat) (Porter 1951). Bands or families of the St. Johns Mikasuki could have migrated into southern Florida in the same manner as the "Tallassays" of the Prince diary. Second, the Gulf coastal swamps were inhabited by the Mikasuki Sam Jones and his followers, who are known eventually to have settled deep in the Everglades. A further complication arises when it is noted that the assemblage from the Weekiwachee site (see chapter 4), possibly attributable to one of these coastal-dwelling Mikasuki bands, contains what appears to be Chattahoochee Brushed pottery and an incised cazuela bowl similar to the Lamar pottery of the Creeks. Thus it is probable that Mikasukis and Tallassees made and used the same type of pottery. Finally, we do not know conclusively what happened to all of the Mikasukis known to have been in the Withlacoochee area, and again, families or bands may have made their way from here south. As any or all of these three source populations may also have provided the ancestry of the present Mikasuki-speaking Seminoles (all reservations except Brighton), the Miccosukees' claim to having an independent history may gain its evidence best through a direct historical approach based on precise genealogical information. In this way, domestic sites associated with known Miccosukees, once located and excavated, may be shown to correlate with known historical events or may be dated by means of archaeological seriation and, thus characterized, may yield an archaeological signature that is distinctly Miccosukee. This conjunctive approach can only proceed once all lines of evidence—genealogical, archaeological, and historical—are known to exist and can be made available. It will be a serious scholarly pursuit not likely to be undertaken by qualified personnel without full assurances from the Miccosukees that the project will be allowed to reach completion. The potential for a Miccosukee archaeology (or history) rests with the Miccosukee themselves, and the degree to which they wish their historical claims to be validated in Western terms.

Final Considerations

Lately, a call has come from various quarters (Miller 1980, Schmidt 1983, Doyel 1982, Kirch 1985) for an archaeology more

attuned to native concepts of history. In the Seminole case, as in
that of most nonliterate societies, until very recent times tribal
histories were preserved through oral means—myths, traditions, and folktales—and were embodied in the drama of ritual
and ceremony. Therefore it is incumbent upon the archaeologist
to become familiar with native methods of historiography and
thereby to derive directions for research on the basis of native
determinations of historical significance.

Unfortunately, Seminole oral histories are becoming fewer
with the passage of each year and are valued not as history but
as entertainment (King 1978:7, 10, 11). In their place, historically
inclined Seminoles can seek out the same textual histories that
are available to the general public (the Seminole libraries at
Brighton and Big Cypress list a number of books pertaining to
Indian history and culture), but these express, unavoidably, a
non-Indian point of view. The Seminole will therefore come to
share the historical perspectives of the majority. However, there
are at least four ways in which archaeological research and traditional native historical concerns can be integrated.

First, there is the matter of the origins of the Florida Seminoles. The "old stories" of the Seminoles and Miccosukees refer
to their western origins (as do many origin myths of the southeastern Indians), yet few Indians possess any additional knowledge. Some are actively unhappy about the vague nature of the
origin stories and would like more detailed information. Such is
the case with the Miccosukees. Therefore, research may be prof-
itably directed toward the identification of modern tribal polities
in the archaeological record. Such identification will require establishing a complex chain of association between material culture, ethnic boundaries, and modern political entities. Should
such associations exist, the history of Florida's extant native
Americans will be greatly enhanced through archaeological
means.

The relationship between the Seminoles and the aboriginal
tribes of Florida is the source of some confusion in the oral record. Some persons claim great antiquity in Florida for their
ancestors (Sturtevant 1971:120; King 1978:63), while others flatly
deny any connection with the Florida aborigines ("Injuns all

dead," Robert Osceola told naturalist Charles Barney Cory. "In-juns came in canoe, eat oysters, play ball"; see Cory 1896:12). There are indeed significant lacunae in the ethnohistorical record with respect to the fates of many of the Florida natives during the late 1600s and early 1700s, the time when the Seminoles began their colonization of Florida. All the oral accounts may thus be true. Some bands may have assimilated the remnants of earlier populations (Cowkeeper of the Alachua savanna clearly did so), while other, and presumably later, Seminole bands did not. Archaeology may permit more precise interpretations of the relationship between the Seminoles and the original Floridians (the Creeks had a major role in their extinction, but was this also the case for the early Seminoles?) if contact sites can be located. The Alachua area, in the vicinity of Paynes Prairie and north of present Gainesville near the former mission site at Fox Pond (the archaeological site of A-272; see Mykel 1962), seems potential in this regard.

The fourth concern is with the archaeological documentation of the evolution of cultural institutions and practices with which the Seminoles of today are familiar. The Seminoles are interested in talking about the origins of the familiar pole and thatch chickee, the types of buildings that were used by nineteenth-century Seminoles and their construction, the way in which camps were organized, and the like. An archaeologist would gather this sort of information regardless of his or her research objectives, and it would need only to be presented in the proper way to the proper audience. To the extent that native concepts of history may dissolve within the next decade, the above concerns may be moot. However, some of the Seminoles might also be expected to want to identify their heritage, preserve it in some fashion, and pass it on to the next generation. In that case, they may turn to archaeologists to provide them with the facts of culture history.

A final consideration relates to the archaeology of the "Semi-nole blacks," primarily runaway slaves and their descendants, who sought out remote regions of the Florida wilderness as a haven for their freedom. I have only briefly mentioned them in this book, notably the band associated with Sitarkey who settled on Boggy (now Kettle) Island on the Withlacoochee, those associated with Micanopy who lived in their own town of Pilaklikaha, and the fearsome groups residing on the middle and lower Gulf coasts, far from the reach of colonial government. The peculiar form of vassalage that existed between the blacks and the Seminoles is not well understood. In the words of a chronicler of the day, the Seminoles were held to be "poor agriculturists and husbandmen, and withal too indolent to till the ground, and, without the negroes, would literally starve" (Potter 1836:45). This popular view continues to be expressed in recent times (Craig and Peebles 1974). The blacks were also greatly trusted by the Seminoles, who used them as interpreters during important treaties and other negotiations. For this reason, captured blacks made ideal informants as to Indian activities and were often used by the army for this purpose (hence Ansel's guiding of Prince to the site of Powell's Town). To judge from the documents of the day, the Seminoles apparently felt that they owned the blacks (and wanted monetary compensation should they have to forfeit the blacks as they were asked to do under American rule), but it is not clear that this concept of ownership was comparable to Western notions of slavery. Blacks were allowed to live separately and often at great distance from the Seminoles, but apparently they did, at least upon occasion, furnish them with a portion of their harvest. What did the Seminoles do for the blacks? The answer may be forthcoming when excavations are undertaken at Kettle Island, Pilaklikaha, and other black settlements in northern peninsular Florida.

Notes

Preface

1. Excerpt from an article by Barbara Billie that appeared in the *Seminole Tribune* of December 30, 1985 (vol.11, no.14) entitled "Miccosukee Swearing In Ceremonies Held."

1. Introduction

1. The Southeast Archeological Center of the National Park Service has made an archaeological survey of Seminole sites in the Big Cypress region of southern Florida. See Ehrenhard, Taylor, and Komara 1980.

2. A summation of Seminole claims and the history of their litigation can be found in the section entitled "Commission Findings" by the Indian Claims Commission, in Fairbanks 1974.

3. The Fairbanks report to the Indian Claims Commission was entered as Docket 73 and was published in 1974 (Fairbanks 1974). The commission's findings of fact were published in the same volume.

4. For Goggin's testimony before the Indian Claims Commission, see Goggin 1963.

5. Primary documents relating to the claims of the Seminole Nation of Oklahoma, Seminole Tribe of Florida, Miccosukee Tribe of Florida, and the unaffiliated Seminoles were compiled and published in 1978 by the U.S. Government Printing Office, Washington, D.C., as *Distribution of Seminole Judgement Funds*.

6. Data provided by the Seminole and Miccosukee tribes and published in the 1981 *Atlas of Florida* include the following figures for the various reservations (population and tribal affiliation in parentheses): Big Cypress (Seminole, 376), Brighton (Seminole, 332), Hollywood (Seminole, 375), Immokalee (Seminole, 27), Forty Mile Bend (Miccosukee, 205). These do not represent total population figures for the Seminoles or Miccosukees.

7. Goggin foresaw this eventuality in 1957; see his letter of March 25 to attorney Paul Nieball (Fairbanks n.d.).

8. A brief version of the Fairbanks taxonomy also appears in chapter 10 of Milanich and Fairbanks (1980).

9. The chronicle of Milfort (1972) is particularly notable in this regard. However, Milfort had a distinct animosity for one William Augustus Bowles, who in the early 1790s attempted to induce certain Seminoles to challenge the balance of power in the Southeast. Swan, writing during the same era, makes the following interesting comment: "They [the Creeks] believe there is a state of future existence, and that according to the tenor of their lives, they shall hereafter be rewarded with the privilege of hunting in the realms of the Master of Breath, or of becoming Seminolies in the region of the old sorceror [evil spirit]" (Swan, in Schoolcraft 1851–1857:vol. 5:270).

10. See note 5 above.

11. See note 6 above.

12. John M. Goggin of the University of Florida was a long-time student of the Florida Seminoles and a leading figure in Seminole archaeology. Unfortunately his early death in 1963 left much of his research in note and manuscript form. Much of his material is now housed at the P. K. Yonge Library of Florida History, Gainesville.

13. The opinion that the Seminoles depended on blacks was also expressed by Woodburne Potter (1836:45), an eyewitness to and chronicler of the Second Seminole War.

2. Antecedents: The Ancestral Creek Pattern

1. The relationship between sacred or "new" fire ceremonies and

mound building is suggested, for instance, by the archaeology of the Citico mound in Tennessee (Thomas 1894:374).

2. As usual, Bartram's recollection of the use of black drink among the Talahoschte Seminoles on the Suwannee River in 1774 is particularly vivid: "Our chief with the rest of the white people in town took their seats according to order: tobacco and pipes were brought; the calumet was lighted and smoked, circulating according to the usual forms and ceremony; and afterwards black drink conclude the feast. The king conversed, drank cassine [black drink], and associated familiarly with his people and with us" (1955:200).

3. William Sturtevant (1954:58) has provided an excellent commentary on the ethnohistory of "scratching" in the aboriginal Southeast.

4. The imported European kaolin face pipes popular among the Indians bear an interesting resemblance to the late prehistoric aboriginal smoking pipes in human effigy.

5. The symbolic importance of the panther to the Seminoles has recently attracted public attention with the trial of Seminole Tribal Chairman James E. Billie for the killing of a panther on the Big Cypress Reservation in 1983. Because panthers are listed as an endangered species, state and federal charges were brought against Billie. In his defense, Billie claimed that the killing formed part of Seminole religion and cited the curative properties that the Indians ascribed to the animal, including the use of the claws and tail to alleviate muscle disease and to increase strength and endurance. State charges were dropped, and a mistrial was recently declared in the federal hearing. Southeastern Indian tradition (Adair 1986:33) and recent observations among the Seminoles (Spoehr 1941:16) suggest that medicine men and spiritual leaders were selected from the Panther clan: James Billie in fact presented the skin from the animal he killed to then Miccosukee Tribal Chairman and esteemed medicine man Sonny Billie (the meat was served to a delegation of tribal chiefs visiting James Billie's hunting camp deep in the Big Cypress). The Seminoles also speak of the water-cougar (Hudson 1976:146), an underwater monster that in part resembles a panther.

6. Knight (1985:25, 26) relates an interesting idea regarding the role of the famous Tukabatchee plates in the acculturation between the Creeks of Tukabatchee and a band of Shawnee that took up residence among them in about 1675. He suggests that the plates, pieces of sheet copper that were probably of European origin, were unwittingly unearthed by the Shawnees during the construction of their houses at Tukabatchee and were presented by them to the Creeks as a special gift to seal an al-

liance. The Creeks invested the plates with a great deal of ritual significance and incorporated them into the busk ceremonies (Swanton 1928a:575, 1946:185; and for related information see Nunez 1958:14).

7. Hudson (1976) and Knight (1981) provide good discussions of color symbolism among the southeastern Indians.

8. Creek hunting territories in the Florida peninsula are mentioned in the records of the British Colonial Land Office, for example in a letter from Governor James Grant to the Board of Trade dated January 1772.

3. Colonization, 1716–1767

1. Caleb Swan's remarks on the Seminoles, collected in volume 5 of Schoolcraft's monumental work on the American Indians (Schoolcraft 1851–1857), report a number of allegations regarding Seminole misconduct on the Georgia-Florida border.

2. About Creek squaregrounds Swan observed (in Schoolcraft 1851–1857:vol. 5:265): "Some towns also have the privilege of a covered square, which is nothing more than a loose scaffolding of canes laid on poles over the whole of the area between the house."

3. It can be inferred from Bartram's description of Cuscowilla that his use of the word "habitation" refers not to individual dwellings but to what he recognized as households.

4. This explains the surprise of St. Johns trader Denys Rolle when several warriors brought their wives with them to dine at his table (Rolle 1977:12).

5. There is brief mention of the annual busk by Governor Grant; see Covington 1961:46.

6. Grant included the Florida Indians among the Lower Creeks.

7. Rolle called the Suwannee the "little Savannah" and described the river distance from his point of crossing to White King's town as one mile.

4. Enterprise, 1767–1821

1. The west bank of the St. Johns River became known as the "Indian shore" after the Indians granted lands east of the river to the British in the 1765 Treaty of Picolata.

2. There is some possibility that the founding of Cuscowilla was related to the presumed abandonment of Latchaway following Neatohowki's act of murder there in 1764 (Rolle 1977:48).

3. Cowkeeper told Bartram that the the dying fish and droves of mosquitoes made it necessary to abandon Latchaway; perhaps there has been some change in the ecology of the prairie. However, in 1774 Bartram rode his horse across the prairie trail without difficulty.

4. In a system of matrilineal inheritance, a man acquires rights and property from his mother's brother, who is a member of the mother's lineage, or descent group. See Gough 1961:631 for cross-cultural examples.

5. Available in the Lockey Collection, P. K. Yonge Library of Florida History, Gainesville, under "Tariff for Trade with the Creek Nation, Pensacola, June 1, 1784."

6. Transcriptions of the Dexter correspondence are available in Glunt (1930), Boyd (1958), and DeVane (1979).

7. The activities of these men, reputed to be British agents, were said to threaten American security in the Southeast, hence Jackson's incursion into Spanish Florida.

7. Like Beads on a String: Observations on the Seminole Cosmos

1. Pierce also describes the following scene in the Sanfalasco village: "Dances are held at night on a level hard beaten central spot; males and females move in Indian file around a fire, singing a wild song; there is little diversity in the steps, but the tunes are varied, each dance is terminated by a general whoop. The chief conducted us to a bower, where we were seated with some of the head men, the villagers not engaged in dancing located themselves in an opposite arbor. The young men, unusually dressed and ornamented, had spurs attached to their showy leg moccasins, and with cheeks blackened to represent whiskers, and faces painted, made a ludicrous appearance. Small terrapin shells filled with pebbles affixed to the ankles of the female dancers, were their only instruments of music; much laughter was excited by the dancing and various amusing tricks" (1825:134).

References

Adair, James. 1986 [1930]. *The History of the American Indians*. Edited by S. C. Williams. Promontory Press, New York. Originally published 1775.

Atlas of Florida. 1981. Edited by Edward A. Fernald. Florida State University Foundation, Tallahassee.

Baker, Henry A. 1976. Archaeological Investigations at Fort Cooper, Inverness, Florida. *Florida Department of State, Bureau of Historic Sites and Properties Bulletin* No. 5, pp. 21–46.

Bartram, John. 1942. Diary of a Journey Through the Carolinas, Georgia, and Florida From July 1, 1765, to April 10, 1766. Edited by Francis Harper. *Transactions of the American Philosophical Society* 33 (1).

Bartram, William. 1955. *The Travels of William Bartram*. Edited by Mark van Doren. Dover, New York.

———. 1958. *The Travels of William Bartram*. Edited by Francis Harper. Yale University Press, New Haven.

Billie, Barbara. 1985. Miccosukee Swearing in Ceremonies Held. *Seminole Tribune* 11(14), December 14.

Boyd, Mark F. 1949. Diego Pena's Expedition to Apalachee and Apalachicola in 1716. *Florida Historical Quarterly* 28:1–27.

———. 1955. Asi-Yahola or Osceola. *Florida Historical Quarterly* 32:249–305.

———. 1958. Horatio S. Dexter and Events Leading to the Treaty of Moultrie Creek with the Seminole Indians. *Florida Anthropologist* 11:65–95.

Brain, Jeffrey P. 1979. *Tunica Treasure*. Papers of the Peabody Museum of Archaeology and Ethnology 71. Harvard University, Cambridge.

Brose, David S. 1980. Coe's Landing (8Ja137), Jackson County, Florida: A Fort Walton Campsite on the Apalachicola River. *Florida Department of State Bureau of Historic Sites and Properties Bulletin* 6:1–31.

Brown, James A. 1985. The Mississippian Period. In *Ancient Art of the American Woodland Indians*, edited by David S. Brose, James A. Brown, and David W. Penney, pp. 93–146. Harry N. Abrams, New York.

Bullen, Ripley. 1950. An Archaeological Survey of the Chattahoochee River Valley in Florida. *Journal of the Washington Academy of Sciences* 40:101–125.

Bushnell, Amy. 1978. "That Demonic Game": The Campaign to Stop Indian Pelota Playing in Spanish Florida, 1675–1684. *Americas* 35(1):1–19.

Buswell, James Oliver III. 1972. *Florida Seminole Religious Ritual: Resistance and Change*. Ph.D. dissertation. St. Louis University, St. Louis, Mo. University Microfilms, Ann Arbor, Michigan.

Caldwell, Joseph R. 1955. Investigations at Rood's Landing, Stewart County, Georgia. *Early Georgia* 2(1):22–49.

Capron, Louis. 1953. The Medicine Bundles of the Florida Seminole and the Green Corn Dance. *Bureau of American Ethnology Bulletin 151, Anthropological Paper* No. 35, pp. 155–210.

———. 1956. Notes on the Hunting Dance of the Cow Creek Seminole. *Florida Anthropologist* 9:67–78.

Clarke, N. S. 1841. Scouting on the Withlacoochee. Keenan-Brown manuscript collection, P. K. Yonge Library of Florida History, Gainesville.

Clausen, Carl J. 1970. The Fort Pierce Collection. *Florida Department of State, Bureau of Historic Sites and Properties Bulletin* No. 1, pp. 1–21.

Cohen, M. M. 1836. *Notices of Florida and the Campaigns*. Burges and Honour, Charleston.

Cory, Charles B. 1896. *Hunting and Fishing in Florida, Including a Key to the Water Birds of the State*. Estes and Lauriat, Boston.

Covington, James W. 1961. *The British Meet the Seminoles*. Contributions of the Florida State Museum, Social Sciences, No. 7. Gainesville.

Craig, Alan K., and Christopher Peebles. 1974. Ethnoecologic Change Among the Seminoles, 1740–1840. *Geoscience and Man* 5:83–96.

DeJarnette, David L. 1975. *Archaeological Salvage in the Walter F. George Basin of the Chattahoochee River in Alabama*. University of Alabama Press, University.

DeJarnette, David L., and Asael T. Hansen. 1960. *The Archaeology of the Childersburg Site, Alabama*. Notes in Anthropology 4. Florida State University, Tallahassee.

DeVane, Park. 1979. *Early Florida History*. Vol. 2. Sebring Historical Society. Copy in P. K. Yonge Library of Florida History, Gainesville.

Dickens, Roy S., Jr. 1979. *Archaeological Investigations at Horseshoe Bend*. Special Publication No. 3. Alabama Archaeological Society, University.

Dickinson, Martin F., and Lucy B. Wayne. 1985. *Archaeological Mitigation of Two Seminole Sites in Marion County, Florida*. Water and Air Research, Gainesville.

Doster, James F. 1974. *The Creek Indians and Their Florida Lands, 1740–1823*. Vols. 1 and 2. Garland Publishing, New York.

Dowd, John T. 1980. The Investigations of the Vandalized Graves of Two Historic Personages: Osceola, Seminole War Chief, and Colonel William M. Shy, Civil War Hero. *Tennessee Anthropologist* 5:47–72.

Doyel, David. 1982. Medicine Men, Ethnic Significance, and Cultural Resource Management. *American Antiquity* 47:634–642.

Ehrenhard, John E., Robert Taylor, and Gregory Komara. 1980. *Big Cypress National Preserve, Cultural Resource Inventory, Season 4*. Southeast Archaeological Center, National Park Service, Tallahassee, Florida.

Evans, Hedvig Tetans. 1978. Seminole Folktales. *Florida Historical Quarterly* 56:473–494.

Evans-Pritchard, E. E. 1940. *The Nuer: A Description of the Modes of Livelihood and Political Institutions of a Nilotic People*. Clarendon Press, Oxford.

Fabel, Robin. 1974. Lieutenant Thomas Campbell's Sojourn among the Creeks, November 1764–May 1765. *Alabama Historical Quarterly* 36:97–111.

Fagan, Brian M. 1986. *People of the Earth*. Little, Brown, Boston.

Fairbanks, Charles H. 1942. The Taxonomic Position of Stallings Island, Georgia. *American Antiquity* 7:223–231.

———. 1956. *Archeology of the Funeral Mound, Ocmulgee National Monument, Georgia*. National Park Service Archaeologial Research Series No. 3. Department of the Interior, Washington, D.C.

———. 1962. Excavations at Horseshoe Bend, Alabama. *Florida Anthropologist* 15:41–56.

———. 1974. *Ethnohistorical Report of the Florida Indians*. Garland Publishing, New York. (Identical to the 1957 presentation before the Indian Claims Commission, Dockets 73, 151).

———. 1978. The Ethno-Archeology of the Florida Seminole. In *Tacachale: Essays on the Indians of Florida and Southeast Georgia during the Historic Period*, edited by Jerald T. Milanich and Samuel Proctor, pp. 163–193. University Presses of Florida, Gainesville.

———. n.d. Fairbanks Manuscript Collection. James Ford Library, Florida State Museum, Gainesville.

Ferguson, George R. 1976. The Weekiwachee Site, Hernando County, Florida. *Florida Anthropologist* 29:69–83.

Florida Folklife Programs. 1984. *Four Corners of Earth*. White Springs, Fl. A video documentary on Seminole women.

Florida Herald. 1836. [Accounts of the Second Seminole War.] January 13, May 12. St. Augustine. Available on microfilm, P. K. Yonge Library of Florida History, Gainesville.

Fogelson, Raymond. 1971. The Cherokee Ballgame Cycle: An Ethnographer's View. *Ethnomusicology* 15:327–338.

Fundaburke, Emma Lila. 1958. *Southeastern Indians, Life Portraits: A Catalogue of Pictures, 1564–1860*. E. L. Fundaburke, Luverne, Ala.

Garbarino, Merwyn S. 1972. *Big Cypress: A Changing Seminole Community*. Holt, Rinehart and Winston, New York.

Gatschet, Albert S. 1884. *A Migration Legend of the Creek Indians*. D. G. Brinton, Philadelphia.

Gluckman, Stephen J., and Christopher Peebles. 1974. Oven Hill (Di-15), A Refuse Site in the Suwannee River. *Florida Anthropologist* 27:21–31.

Glunt, James. 1930. Plantation and Frontier Records of East and Middle Florida. Ph.D. dissertation. University of Michigan, Ann Arbor.

Goggin, John M. 1951. Beaded Shoulder Pouches of the Florida Seminole. *Florida Anthropologist* 4:3–17.

———. 1953. Seminole Archaeology in East Florida. *Southeastern Archaeological Conference Newsletter* 3(3):16, 19.

———. 1958. Seminole Pottery. In *Prehistoric Pottery of the Eastern United States*. Museum of Anthropology, University of Michigan, Ann Arbor.

———. 1963. *Before the Indian Claims Commission*. U.S. Government Printing Office, Washington, D.C.

————. n.d. Goggin notecard collection. Indexed boxes. P. K. Yonge Library of Florida History, Gainesville.

Goggin, John M., Mary E. Godwin, Earl Hester, David Prange, and Robert Spangenberg. 1949. A Historic Indian Burial, Alachua County, Florida. *Florida Anthropologist* 2:10–24.

Gough, Kathleen. 1961. The Modern Disintegration of Matrilineal Descent Groups. In *Matrilineal Kinship*, edited by David M. Schneider and Kathleen Gough, pp. 631–652. University of California Press, Berkeley.

Grant, James [Governor of East Florida]. 1772. Letters [transcriptions]. Bound copy entitled "Records of the British Colonial Land Office." Copy in the University of Florida Library, Gainesville.

Green, Michael D. 1980. Alexander McGillivray. In *American Indian Leaders*, edited by R. David Edmunds, pp. 41–63. University of Nebraska Press, Lincoln.

Greenlee, Robert F. 1944. Medicine and Curing Practices of the Modern Seminole. *American Anthropologist* 46:317–328.

Gregory, Hiram A., and Clarence H. Webb. 1965. European Trade Beads from Six Sites in Natchitoches Parish, Louisiana. *Florida Anthropologist* 18:15–44.

Griffin, John. 1957. Some Comments on the Seminole in 1818. *Florida Anthropologist* 10:41–49.

Haas, Mary R. 1971. Southeastern Indian Linguistics. In *Red, White and Black: Symposium on Indians in the Old South*, edited by Charles M. Hudson, pp. 44–54. University of Georgia Press, Athens.

Hall, Robert L. 1977. An Anthropocentric Perspective for Eastern United States Prehistory. *American Antiquity* 42:499–518.

Hally, David J. 1986. The Identification of Vessel Function: A Case Study From Northwest Georgia. *American Antiquity* 51:267–295.

Hammond, E. A. 1973. The Spanish Fisheries of Charlotte Harbor. *Florida Historical Quarterly* 51:355–380.

Hawkins, Benjamin. 1980. *Letters, Journals, and Writings of Benjamin Hawkins. Vol. 1: 1796–1801*. Edited by C. L. Grant. Beehive Press, Savannah.

Hitchcock, Ethan Allen. 1930. *A Traveler in Indian Territory: The Journal of Ethan Allen Hitchcock, Late Major General in the United States Army*. Edited and annotated by Grant Foreman. Torch Press, Cedar Rapids.

Hodder, Ian. 1982. *Symbols in Action*. Cambridge University Press, London.

Howard, James H. 1968. *The Southeastern Ceremonial Complex and Its*

Interpretation. Missouri Archaeological Society Memoirs No. 6, Columbia.

Hudson, Charles M. 1976. *The Southeastern Indians*. The University of Tennessee Press, Knoxville.

Hudson, Charles M., M. Smith, D. Hally, R. Polhemus, and C. De-Pratter. 1985. Coosa: A Chiefdom in the Sixteenth-Century Southeastern United States. *American Antiquity* 5:723–737.

Hume, Ivor Noel. 1972. *A Guide to Artifacts of Colonial America*. Alfred A. Knopf, New York.

Jesup, Thomas S. 1837. Letters sent, February 7–May 8, 1837. Headquarters, Army of the South. Record Group 94. Records of the Adjutant General's Office. National Archives, Washington, D.C.

King, R. T. 1978. The Florida Seminole Polity, 1858–1978. Ph.D. dissertation. University of Florida, Gainesville.

Kirch, Patrick V. 1985. *The Evolution of the Polynesian Chiefdoms*. Cambridge University Press, Cambridge.

Knight, Vernon J., Jr. 1981. Mississippian Religion. Ph.D. dissertation. University of Florida, Gainesville.

———. 1985. *Tukabatchee: Archaeological Investigations at an Historic Creek Town, Elmore County, Alabama, 1984*. Report of Investigations 45. University of Alabama, Office of Archaeological Research, University.

———. 1986. The Institutional Organization of Mississippian Religion. *American Antiquity* 51:675–687.

Lewis, Kenneth E., Jr. 1969. History and Archeology of Spalding's Lower Store (Pu-23), Putnam County, Florida. M.A. thesis. University of Florida, Gainesville.

Lewis, Thomas M. N., and Madeline Kneberg. 1946. *Hiwassee Island: An Archaeological Account of Four Tennessee Indian Peoples*. University of Tennessee Press, Knoxville.

Lien, Paul. 1986. A Spontoon Tomahawk from Dixie County. *Florida Anthropologist* 39:224–225.

Lockey, Joseph B. 1945. *East Florida, 1783–1785*. University of California Press, Berkeley.

———. n.d. Manuscripts and notes [Tariff for Trade with the Creek Nation]. P. K. Yonge Library of Florida History, Gainesville.

Lorant, Stefan. 1946. *The New World: The First Pictures of America*. Duell, Sloan, and Pearce, New York.

MacCauley, Clay. 1887. The Seminole Indians of Florida. In *Fifth Annual Report of the Bureau of Ethnology*, pp. 469–531. Washington, D.C.

Mahon, John K. 1967. *History of the Second Seminole War*. University of Florida Press, Gainesville.

Mathiessen, Peter. 1984. *Indian Country*. Viking Press, New York.

Milanich, Jerald T., and Charles H. Fairbanks. 1980. *Florida Archaeology*. Academic Press, New York.

Milfort, Le Clerc. 1972. *Memoirs; or A Quick Glance at my Various Travels and My Sojourn in the Creek Nation*. Translated and edited by Ben C. McCary. Beehive Press, Savannah.

Miller, Christopher L., and George R. Hamell. 1986. A New Perspective on Indian-White Contact: Cultural Symbols and Colonial Trade. *Journal of American History* 73:311–328.

Miller, Daniel. 1980. Archaeology and Development. *Current Anthropology*. 21:709–727.

Mitchem, Jeffrey M., and Dale L. Hutchinson. 1986. *Interim Report on Excavations at the Tatham Mound*. Miscellaneous Project Report Series 28. Florida State Museum, Gainesville.

Mitchem, Jeffrey M., Brent R. Weisman, Donna L. Ruhl, Jenette Savell, Laura Sellers, and Lisa Sharik. 1985. *Preliminary Report on Excavations at the Tatham Mound (8Ci203), Citrus County, Florida: Season 1*. Miscellaneous Project Report Series 23. Florida State Museum, Gainesville.

Muller, Jon. 1987. Salt, Chert, and Shell: Mississippian Exchange and Economy. In *Specialization, Exchange, and Complex Societies*, edited by Elizabeth M. Brumfiel and Timothy K. Earle, pp. 10–21. Cambridge University Press, Cambridge.

Mullins, Sue Ann. 1978. Archaeological Survey and Excavations in the Payne's Prairie State Preserve. M.A. thesis. University of Florida, Gainesville.

Mykel, Nancy. 1962. Seminole Sites in Alachua County. Manuscript. Copy in Department of Anthropology, Florida State Museum, Gainesville.

Neill, Wilfred T. 1955. The Identity of Florida's "Spanish Indians." *Florida Anthropologist* 8:43–57.

Nunez, Theron. 1958. Creek Nativism and the Creek War of 1813–1814. *Ethnohistory* 5:1–47, 131–175, 292–301.

Olsen, Stanley. 1963. Dating Early Plain Buttons by Their Form. *American Antiquity* 28:551–554.

Olsen, Stanley, and J.D. Campbell. 1962. Uniform Buttons as Interpretive Aids for Military Sites. *Curator* 5:346–352.

Ortiz, Alfonso. 1972. Ritual Drama and the Pueblo World View. In *New Perspectives on the Pueblos*, edited by Alfonso Ortiz, pp. 135–161. University of New Mexico Press, Albuquerque.

Pierce, James. 1825. Notices of the Agriculture, Scenery, Geology, and Animal, Vegetable, and Mineral Productions of the Floridas, And of the Indian Tribes, Made During A Recent Tour In These Countries. *American Journal of Science*, ser. 1, 9:119–136.

Piper, Harry M., Kenneth W. Hardin, and Jacquelyn G. Piper. 1982. Cultural Responses to Stress: Patterns Observed in American Indian Burials of the Second Seminole War. *Southeastern Archaeology* 1:122–137.

Piper, Harry M., and Jacquelyn G. Piper. 1982. *Archaeological Excavations at the Quad Block Site, 8Hi998*. Piper Archaeological Research, St. Petersburg, Florida.

Pope, John. 1979. [1792.] *A Tour Through The Southern And Western Territories of the United States of North America*. Facsimile reproduction. University Presses of Florida, Gainesville.

Porter, Kenneth W. 1943. Florida Slaves and Free Negroes in the Seminole War, 1835–1842. *Journal of Negro History* 28(4):390–421.

———. 1951. Origins of the St. John's River Seminole: Were They Mikasuki? *Florida Anthropologist* 4(3–4):39–45.

Potter, Woodburne. 1836. *The War in Florida, Being an Exposition of its Causes and an Accurate History of the Campaigns of Generals Clinch, Gaines, and Scott*. Lewis and Coleman, Baltimore.

Prentice, Guy. 1986. An Analysis of the Symbolism Expressed by the Birger Figurine. *American Antiquity* 51:239–266.

Prince, Henry. 1836–1842. The Prince diary. Manuscript and transcription by Frank Laumer. P. K. Yonge Library of Florida History, Gainesville.

———. 1837. Map no. 3. Record Group 94. Records of Adjutant General's Office. National Archives, Washington, D.C.

Recollections of a Campaign in Florida. 1845–1846. *Yale Literary Magazine* 11(1–3):72, 130. Available on microfilm, P. K. Yonge Library of Florida History, Gainesville.

Rolle, Denys. 1977. *The Humble Petition of Denys Rolle*. University Presses of Florida, Gainesville. Originally published 1765.

Rowles, W. P. 1841. Incidents and Observations in Florida in 1836. *Southron*, p. 54ff. Copy in P. K. Yonge Library of Florida History, Gainesville.

Scarry, John. 1984. *Fort Walton Development: Mississippian Chiefdoms in the Lower Southeast*. University Microfilms, Ann Arbor.

Schmidt, Peter R. 1983. An Alternative to a Strictly Materialist Perspective: A Review of Historical Archaeology, Ethnoarchaeology, and Symbolic Approaches in African Archaeology. *American Antiquity* 48:62–79.

Schnell, Frank T. 1970. A Comparative Study of Some Lower Creek Sites. *Southeastern Archaeological Conference Bulletin* 13:133–136.

Schnell, Frank T., Vernon J. Knight, Jr., and Gail S. Schnell. 1981. *Cemochechobee, Archaeology of a Mississippian Ceremonial Center on the Chattahoochee River*. University Presses of Florida, Gainesville.

Sears, William H. 1955. Creek and Cherokee Culture in the Eighteenth Century. *American Antiquity* 21:143–149.

———. 1959. A-296—A Seminole Site in Alachua County. *Florida Anthropologist* 7:25–30.

Skinner, Alanson. 1913. Notes on the Florida Seminole. *American Anthropologist* 15:63–77.

Smith, Hale G. 1948. Two Historical Archaeological Periods In Florida. *American Antiquity* 4:313–319.

Smith, Marvin T. 1979. Glass Trade Beads from Nuyaka. In *Archaeological Investigations at Horseshoe Bend*, edited by Roy S. Dickens, Jr., pp. 166–170. Special Publication. Alabama Archaeological Society, University.

———. 1987. *Archaeology of Aboriginal Culture Change in the Interior Southeast: Depopulation during the Early Historic Period*. University Presses of Florida, Gainesville.

Spoehr, Alexander. 1941. Camp, Clan, and Kin among the Cow Creek Seminole of Florida. *Field Museum of Natural History Anthropological Series* 22(1):1–27.

———. 1944. The Florida Seminole Camp. *Field Museum of Natural History Anthropological Series* 33(3):117–150.

Stirling, Gene. 1935. *Report on the Seminole Indians of Florida*. Office of Indian Affairs, Applied Anthropology Unit, Washington, D.C.

Sturtevant, William C. 1953. Chakaika and the "Spanish Indians": Documentary Sources Compared with Seminole Tradition. *Tequesta* 13:35–73.

———. 1954. The Medicine Bundles and Busks of the Florida Seminole. *Florida Anthropologist* 7:31–70.

———. 1962. A Newly Discovered 1838 Drawing of a Seminole Dance. *Florida Anthropologist* 15:73–80.

———. 1971. Creek into Seminole. In *North American Indians in Historical Perspective*, edited by Eleanor Burke Leacock and Nancy Oestreich Lurie, pp. 92–128. Random House, New York.

Swan, Caleb. 1795. Position and State of Manners and Arts in the Creek, or Muscogee Nation in 1791. In *Information Respecting the History, Condition, And Prospects of the Indian Tribes of the United States,* vol. 5, by Henry Rowe Schoolcraft, 1851–1857. Lippincott and Grambo, Philadelphia.

Swanton, John R. 1922. *Early History of the Creek Indians and Their Neighbors*. Bureau of American Ethnology Bulletin No. 73. Smithsonian Institution, Washington, D.C.

———. 1928a. Religious Beliefs and Medical Practices of the Creek Indians. *Bureau of American Ethnology Annual Report* No. 42, pp. 477–672.

———. 1928b. Social Organization and Social Usages of the Indians of the Creek Confederacy. *Bureau of American Ethnology Annual Report* No. 42, pp. 23–472.

———. 1928c. The Interpretation of Aboriginal Mounds by Means of Creek Indian Customs. *Annual Report of the Smithsonian Institution*, 1927:495–507. Washington, D.C.

———. 1932. The Green Corn Dance. *Chronicles of Oklahoma* 10:170–195.

———. 1946. *Indians of the Southeastern United States*. Bureau of American Ethnology Bulletin 137. Smithsonian Institution, Washington, D.C.

Thomas, Cyrus. 1894. Report on the Mound Exploration of the Bureau of American Ethnology. *Bureau of American Ethnology Annual Report* No. 12.

Thurman, Melburn D. 1977. Seminoles, Creeks, Delawares, and Shawnees: Indian Auxiliaries in the Second Seminole War. *Florida Anthropologist* 30:144–165.

Wallace, Anthony F. C. 1956. Revitalization Movements. *American Anthropologist* 58:264–281.

Ward, Mary McNeer. 1955. The Disappearance of the Head of Osceola. *Florida Historical Quarterly* 33:193–201.

Waring, Antonio J., Jr. 1968. The Southern Cult and Muskhogean Ceremonial: General Considerations. In *The Waring Papers*, edited by Stephen Williams. Papers of the Peabody Museum of Archaeology and Ethnology 58:87–93. Harvard University, Cambridge.

Waring, Antonio J., Jr., and Preston Holder. 1945. A Prehistoric Ceremonial Complex in the Southeastern United States. *American Anthropologist* 47:1–34.

Waselkov, Gregory A. 1985. Upper Creek Faunal Exploitation. In *Culture Change on the Creek Frontier*, edited by Gregory A. Waselkov, pp. 79–88. Final Report to the National Science Foundation, Grant Award BNS-830547. Auburn University, Auburn, Alabama.

Waselkov, Gregory A., and R. Eli Paul. 1981. Frontiers and Archaeology. *North American Archaeologist* 2:309–329.

Wauchope, Robert. 1966. *Archaeological Survey of Northern Georgia*. Memoir No. 21. Society for American Archaeology, Salt Lake City.

Weisman, Brent R. 1983. *The Search for Powell's Town: A Preliminary Report on Survey and Test Excavations*. Miscellaneous Project Report Series 19. Florida State Museum, Gainesville.

―――. 1985a. Some Notes on the Fort Brooke Cemetery. Florida Anthropological Society *Newsletter* 106:4–5.

―――. 1985b. *The Cove of the Withlacoochee Archaeology Project, Final Compliance Report*. Miscellaneous Project Report Series 24. Florida State Museum, Gainesville.

―――. 1986a. Newman's Garden (8Ci206): A Seminole Indian Site near Lake Tsala Apopka, Florida. *Florida Anthropologist* 39:208–220.

―――. 1986b. The Cove of the Withlacoochee: A First Look at the Archaeology of an Interior Florida Wetland. *Florida Anthropologist* 39:4–23.

―――. 1987. On the Trail of Osceola's Seminoles in Florida. *Archaeology* 40 (2):58–59.

Welch, Andrew. 1977. *A Narrative of the Early Days and Remembrances of Oceola Nikkanochee, Prince of Econchatti*. University Presses of Florida, Gainesville. Originally published, 1841.

Wenke, Robert J. 1980. *Patterns in Prehistory*. Oxford University Press, New York.

Wickman, Patricia R. 1986. The Material Legacy of Osceola. M.A. thesis, University of Florida, Gainesville.

Wienker, Curtis W. 1982. The Human Remains from 8Hi998. In *Archaeological Excavations at the Quad Block Site, 8Hi998*, edited by Harry M. Piper and Jacquelyn G. Piper. Piper Archaeological Research, St. Petersburg, Florida.

Willey, Gordon R. 1949. *Archaeology of the Florida Gulf Coast*. Smithsonian Miscellaneous Collections 113. Smithsonian Institution, Washington, D.C.

Williams, Mark, and Gary Shapiro. 1986. Shoulderbone Was a Fourteenth Century Frontier Town. *LAMAR Briefs* 8:6.

Willoughby, Charles C. 1932. History and Symbolism of the Muskhogeans and the People of Etowah. In *Etowah Papers*, edited by Warren K. Moorehead, pp. 7–67. Yale University Press, New Haven.

Witthoft, John. 1949. *Green Corn Ceremonialism in the Eastern Woodlands*. Occasional Paper from the Museum of Anthropology, University of Michigan, No. 13. University of Michigan Press, Ann Arbor.

Wright, J. Leitch, Jr. 1986. *Creeks and Seminoles*. University of Nebraska Press, Lincoln.

Wyckoff, Martin A. 1984. *United States Military Buttons of the Land Services 1787 1902*. McClean County Historical Society, Bloomington, Illinois.

Young, Hugh. 1934–1935. A Topographic Memoire on East and West Florida With Itineraries of General Jackson's Army, 1818. *Florida Historical Quarterly* 13:16–50, 82–104, 129–164.

Index